"Finally, in *Get Me Carlucci*, one of the most talented, effective and courageous people ever to serve in multiple high government offices gets due recognition. From my perch on the National Security Staff at the White House and at CIA, I witnessed Frank Carlucci as US ambassador play a critical role in bringing about Portugal's transition from dictatorship to democracy in the mid-1970s, bring common sense and effective leadership to reform of the CIA and the intelligence community as deputy director of Central Intelligence under Jimmy Carter, restore confidence in the Reagan NSC as national security adviser after the Iran-Contra scandal, and lead the Defense Department at the end of the Cold War. In this book, Kristin Carlucci Weed, Frank's daughter, describes his actions in these and other momentous roles with clarity and honesty, illuminating the extraordinary leadership skills relied upon by multiple presidents of both political parties. A diminutive man with a deceptively easy-going manner and friendly smile, Carlucci possessed an iron will and extraordinary physical and political courage. *Get Me Carlucci* wonderfully portrays one of the most extraordinary men ever to serve the American people."

—Robert M. Gates, former Secretary of Defense (2006–2011), former Director of Central Intelligence (1991–1993)

"Kristin Carlucci Weed's book is important for those who care about true government service. In my years as Frank Carlucci's senior military assistant, I never saw a more dedicated government servant. He cared about our country, the policies for protecting it, and the importance of engagement in a world that needed American engagement so much, and he did it so well. Anyone interested or involved in government service should read and absorb the great lessons from the great man in this book."

—Admiral Bill Owens

"*Get Me Carlucci* is a comprehensive portrait of one of Washington's most influential leaders. During both Republican and Democratic administrations, Secretary Carlucci represented the best of Washington, and this book captures in his own words the legacy of great foreign policy and national security accomplishment he left behind. Drawing upon extensive research into his personal files and writings, *Get Me Carlucci* delivers a portrait of a man who devoted himself to doing what was right for America."

—Stephen J. Hadley, former National Security Advisor

"Frank Carlucci was one of the twentieth century's most influential public figures. This book is an overdue account of his extraordinary career, his contributions to sound public policy, and the many people he touched, all enriched by special insights into his roles as father, husband, and grandfather. A memorable book about a remarkable man."

—Michael Rich, President Emeritus, RAND Corporation

GET ME CARLUCCI

GET ME CARLUCCI

A DAUGHTER RECOUNTS HER FATHER'S LEGACY *of* SERVICE

KRISTIN CARLUCCI WEED
AND FRANK C. CARLUCCI III

DISRUPTION
BOOKS
New York *Austin*

Published by Disruption Books
New York, New York
www.disruptionbooks.com

Distributed by Disruption Books

For information about special discounts for bulk purchases, please contact Disruption Books at info@disruptionbooks.com.

Cover images courtesy of the author and © Shutterstock / RedKoala
Cover and book design by Sheila Parr

Library of Congress Cataloging-in-Publication Data is available
Printed in the United States of America

Print ISBN: 978-1-63331-083-4
eBook ISBN: 978-1-63331-084-1

First Edition

For Joey, Marina, Anna, Amelia, Charlotte, and Greyson.

May you aspire to live a life for the greater good.

CONTENTS

ACKNOWLEDGMENTS

THE IDEA OF TURNING my father's personal memoir into a book didn't come out of the blue. When he first drafted his memoir toward the end of his life, my dad would print out copies and hand them to me, ask me to edit them. At the time, I was newly married, buried deep in my own work as a young professional, and had no interest in helping him with his project. "It's fine, Dad," I said. "Looks good."

How perspective changes with time. How I wish he could see the book we created together.

To that end, I'd like to thank my dad. For his lifetime of public service, but also for teaching me what it means to be a good human. To be humble, to be kind, to serve our country, and to take pleasure in the simple things in life—like a good game of tennis, or a nice glass of red wine. Thanks for joining me in the endeavor, even if you will never know you did.

I am also greatly indebted to my mother, Marcia, who championed the idea of this book and offered up stories of her life and boxes of old photographs, newspaper clippings, and speeches. I know you were glad to get them out of your house. Thank you for letting me record your personal memories on our walks and at my kitchen table, even when it felt awkward to do so.

Thank you to my wonderful husband, Josh, without whose constant love and support nothing in my life is possible. And to my children, Amelia, Charlotte, and Greyson—I love you so much. You are my motivation behind turning a family heirloom into this book. I hope this will help you, and generations after you, remember and learn from your Bumpa's story.

To my brother, Chip, for walking through life with me. From my beginnings on Mintwood Drive, you have always been a protector and supporter of your little sister. For that, I am eternally grateful. And to his family, Yvette, Marina, and Anna; I love you.

Thank you to Shannon O'Neill, editor and writer extraordinaire, without whom this book would be a figment of my imagination. Thank you for believing in this idea from the beginning and shaping it into the book it has become. I enjoyed working with you immensely.

To the strong three-woman team at Disruption Books: Kris Pauls, Alli Shapiro, and Janet Potter; thank you for having faith in me. In particular, thank you to Alli for responding swiftly to any publishing or editorial query I had. Thank you also to Sheila Parr, Julie Mercer Carroll, Kirstin Andrews, Killian Piraro, and Travis Hale. I am grateful.

I am also greatly indebted to all our family, friends, and colleagues who afforded me interviews for this book or helped along the way. Including, but not limited to: Colin Powell, David Rubenstein, William Taft, Grant Green, John Garon, Bill Owens, Michael Rich, Jim Thompson, Susan Davis, Karen Carlucci Romano, and Joan Kleinrock.

PREFACE

FRANK CHARLES CARLUCCI III held many important jobs over the course of his life: Secretary of Defense, National Security Advisor, Deputy Director of the CIA, Ambassador to Portugal. But to me, he was one thing more: he was my dad.

I came to admire and respect the many roles he performed and his service to the country. But I have to admit, as a young person, I didn't dwell too much on the positions my father held. I always knew my father was hardworking and dedicated. I saw it with my own eyes as he labored late into the night in his leather chair in our downstairs den, the TV in the corner tuned to the news and his one glass of red wine on the desk beside him. I saw it in how he was frequently called to Capitol Hill (and sometimes to places much farther away) for urgent business on short notice. I didn't know he was preparing for meetings with the president, where they would work together on containing the threat posed by the Soviet Union's stockpiling of nuclear weapons during the height of the Cold War. Or that he was crunching the latest budget numbers to see how he could gain support for his plan to close military bases in order to have the funds to help modernize America's armed forces. Or that he was kept up trying to figure out how to respond to a terrorist attack in Libya that killed US citizens.

As a child, all I knew was that sometimes he brought his work home, and sometimes he brought his family to work. My older half brother, Chip, remembers running through the halls and sliding down the banisters of federal buildings on Saturday mornings. By the time I was born, my father had a playpen in his office at the Department of Defense where he used to park me occasionally when I was an infant. Once in a while General Colin Powell, then national security advisor, was asked to stop in and moonlight as my babysitter. I grew up hearing about my father's early adventures in far-flung locales, but he always downplayed his own role in these stories, even if he was truly in the center of the action: "a small, wiry, engaging dynamo," as his friend General Powell called him.

Before he passed away several years ago, my father wrote an account of his career in a short manuscript. Assembled in one place, the story of his life's path was even more remarkable than I'd imagined, with twists and turns, chance encounters, and a serendipitous sequence of events that led to his role as secretary of defense. My father would never have used words like "remarkable," "incredible," or "important" to describe himself or what he had accomplished; he was always understated and direct. But his career was all of these things. And so was he.

When I read the pages he had written, I could hear my father's voice: characteristic deadpan humor, tell-it-like-it-is sensibility, no frills and no fuss. I wanted to keep that voice alive and maintain his firsthand accounts of everything he'd seen and done, all the interactions with people he'd met along the way. I also knew I wanted this book to be more than a family project. I wanted to share his view of history with a broader audience, who I hoped would find it as interesting as I did. But how to fill in the missing pieces? How could I provide more background or context to give a sense of what the scene was like in the early 1960s in the Congo, or in the mid-'70s in Portugal? Or what it meant to have President Kennedy come looking for you while he was in a meeting and you were but a young Foreign Service Officer? Or what it felt like to talk to Richard Nixon in Brazil about devastating flooding in your hometown in Pennsylvania? Or what it took to do damage control when President Reagan decided to go off-script at a summit with the Soviets and declare a sudden plan for disarmament? *The Washington Post* mused about his already lengthy and colorful career in government when my father became deputy secretary of defense in 1981:

> "Get me Carlucci." Presidents Kennedy, Nixon, Ford—and now President-elect Ronald Reagan—have all said that over the last 20 years. That alone qualifies Frank Carlucci III for the title of Washington's ultimate survivor. But his story is more interesting, and more significant than that . . .
>
> Carlucci, 50, has what the Washington mighty perceive as the right stuff for the man behind the boss. How can you explain such moves as these: Chosen by Carter to help [Director] Stanfield Turner slim and cool down the CIA, Carlucci has now been approved by Reagan to help [Secretary of Defense] Caspar W. Weinberger fatten and heat up the Pentagon. After first fighting Weinberger when he was at the old Department of Health, Education and

Welfare in the Nixon years, Carlucci went on to be his deputy there. As US ambassador to Portugal in 1976, Carlucci followed the program for which his predecessor was fired, and succeeded, even though he bucked then Secretary of State Henry A. Kissinger. And, after being stabbed in the Belgian Congo (now Zaire) at one phase in his government career, Carlucci was hailed as a friend of the Congolese at another. How does he do it?[1]

That question is one I want to answer in these pages. In his own short memoir, my father described these experiences and many others at a rapid-fire pace, assuming a lot of the reader in terms of their familiarity with world history, international affairs, and politics. I decided to take on the role of my father's coauthor to make his experiences more understandable to those outside of his inner circle. I felt equipped to do the job, and not just because he was my father. Before I met my husband and my own life path took a happily unexpected turn, I was quite sure I would follow my father into a career in foreign policy. I studied public policy at Duke University and went on to the School for Advanced International Studies (SAIS) at Johns Hopkins University. When I was a young child, my parents would pull me out of school at a moment's notice to travel the world with them, and these trips had a lasting impact on me. Certainly, I learned more from our travels than I would have from whatever lessons I missed during these school absences. Later in my academic studies, I quickly deduced that I didn't have my father's natural knack for acquiring languages (he spoke six, while one foreign language was about all I could master), but I did find that his intense fascination with other cultures and his desire to live and work in other countries played out in my own life as well.

In thinking about this book, I figured I was better equipped than most to be Dad's collaborator. I had studied the context of many of his adventures and spoken with some of his contemporaries. It's difficult to explain how poignant and moving it was to learn more about my father, his work, and the particulars of a time gone by from the people who sat at the next desk over, or who came to annual Christmas parties, or who worked overseas with him. Closer to home, I dug into boxes and binders of newspaper clippings, old photographs, home movies, and memorabilia that my mother and other family members had kept for decades. And then there was the added benefit of learning from my father and hearing his recollections of events directly for the first forty years of my life until he died in 2018.

But when he was here, it wasn't as if he sat me beside him and imparted his wisdom. My father was hard-driving, self-effacing, and whip-smart. He was not effusive with praise or warm in his affect. When he paid you a compliment or told you "well done," you knew he meant it. And it mattered. My father worked hard, held himself to the highest standard, and expected that others do the same. I have done my best to do that in these pages. My goal has been to maintain his view of what he experienced while also giving the reader a sense of the larger landscape around him at the time, in order to better make sense of what he saw and did. Many of these historical moments have been recounted from other vantage points. Though I certainly have done my best to be factually accurate, I am telling Frank Carlucci's side of the story.

I believe that this narrative of my father's career and his life is far more than a collection of family lore. My father was an example of a highly effective nonpartisan leader, one who didn't come from a well-connected or wealthy family. After attending

Princeton, he could have chosen from a multitude of careers, but his chosen path was one of government service. He was not content to coast along as a diplomat or a bureaucrat. Instead, he was at the center of the action everywhere he went.

My father worked with six different presidents but never ran for political office. His motivations were not recognition or personal aggrandizement. I respect and admire that about him, but it's another reason I wanted to write this book: because of my father's low-key nature and his desire to get things done rather than seek the spotlight, his story has in some ways been overshadowed by some of his contemporaries, including those he mentored. It's fascinating to me that my father is still a household name in Portugal, where he served a pivotal role as ambassador during the struggle for Portuguese democracy. And yet, what he did in Portugal and why it had such a lasting impact has never been effectively captured for a wider audience, and here in America his name and his legacy (much of which has nothing at all to do with Portugal!) have been somewhat lost to history. More broadly, the ideal my father epitomized as a representative of a certain sort of Washington figure has largely disappeared from the highly partisan American political landscape of today. As a country, we would all do better to remember that desire for service before self and party, and to look for leaders today who embody those values. Casper "Cap" Weinberger, his former boss, called him "a true model of quiet, dedicated, brilliant, patriotic service to the nation."[2]

More than anything, I want to share my father's story because it is an American Dream story, almost "Hamiltonian" in nature. My father had one shot, and he knew it. He wasn't going to miss his chance; he was going to take every opportunity he was given and work as hard as he could to fulfill the mandate of his office. In my father's swearing in as secretary of defense, President Reagan said:

> Yes, Frank is the grandson of an Italian stonecutter; he knows in a special way not only what this nation means to all of us but to the entire world. The fact that he's reached the heights he has in his own life says a great deal about him and his family, but it also says something about this great nation and the cause of world freedom for which it stands. Frank Carlucci is living proof to all of us and to the world that "only in America" is more than just an easy cliché: it's a great ringing truth.[3]

❋❋❋

My father was a public and historical figure, but some elements of his work had a far more immediate and personal impact on me. For instance, the memories of when I tagged along on a trip to the USSR in 1990 are still vivid. We stayed just next to the Kremlin in Moscow at a time when very few Westerners were permitted to visit. My father met with Soviet government officials but what I remember is the intense cold, Lenin's tomb at Red Square, and going to the Bolshoi Ballet Academy. I saw children five and six years old performing alongside the adults with incredible skill and precision. I remember being captivated and chilled watching them, these kids just a few years younger than me, who seemed more like smaller cutouts of adults than real live children. They seemed so serious and professional, already set on a strict and straight path toward who they would be for the rest of their lives. On a trip to China, I remember being dragged along to a formal dinner that went so late that I lay down and fell asleep in a long hallway on my walk back from the bathroom. A visit to Morocco went awry when I got food poisoning and felt so awful that I had the hotel call my mother and interrupt an event that she and my father were attending with the royal family.

I remember details like these, mostly specific memories from my father's travels. But it wasn't until I started working on this project, my father's last, that I came to understand a far more complete story of what he had accomplished in his life. The more I learned, the more strongly I felt that this story should be shared with others. In my research I tracked down as many colleagues of my father's as I could: from his time in the Foreign Service, from working at OMB, the CIA, the DoD, from his time as a private sector employee at Sears World Trade and at Carlyle Group, and from places like the global policy think tank RAND, where he served a long tenure on the board. Sadly, many of my father's contemporaries have passed away, including a number of them during the process of composing this book. One was my father's only sibling, my aunt Joan. Another was one of my father's most treasured friends, General Colin Powell. I was honored to be one of the last people outside of his family to speak with him before he died on October 18, 2021. The memories that Powell shared with me helped me gain a better understanding of the unique friendship and working relationship between the general and my father, one that transformed from that of mentee and mentor to equals to a deep and mutual admiration over the years. That last talk I had with Powell will be meaningful to me for the rest of my life.

In this memoir I feel almost as if I am continuing a conversation with my father that I never got a chance to finish. In my role in these pages, I imagine myself as a mediator between the written text he left behind and everything else that he glossed over or hurried through. I worked to splice together his own recollections with more context and backstory, and to fill out the slim portrait of himself that he shared in his own depictions. Since he always shunned the spotlight, I felt it my job to help bring him out of the shadows, to show him in as complete a manner as I could: as a statesman, and as the person and father I knew.

CHAPTER ONE

FIND A WAY *or* MAKE ONE

MY FATHER HAD A lot of admirable qualities. Patience was not one of them. I have little doubt that my father's tendency to move quickly and to always keep his eyes open and his feelings to himself had their origins in his upbringing.

My father, Frank Carlucci III, was born on October 18, 1930, in Scranton, Pennsylvania. His namesake, Frank C. Carlucci I, my great-grandfather, had come to Scranton from Santomenna, Salerno, Italy. He had been a stonecutter in the old country and, after arriving penniless, he worked his way up to become a successful stonemason. My father's parents met at Lafayette College in Easton, Pennsylvania. Frank II was an insurance salesman and a proud businessman. He liked to harangue my father for not going into business—somewhat ironic given the fact that my father did in fact end up as one of the earliest partners of The Carlyle Group, now one of the largest private equity firms in the world, though that element of his career was not the one he dwelled on later in his life.

My father was not a reclusive child, but he was reserved. He'd spend long hours roaming the woods around the family's cabin in Bear Creek, Pennsylvania. His sister, five years younger, was not much of a companion. When my father was ten or eleven, his parents divorced. I don't know what transpired between my grandparents exactly, but divorce was not common at the time, and for Italian immigrants it was practically unheard of. Family ties, always strong in the old country, were now lifelines that kept new immigrants tethered to both their life in a new country and to the traditions and culture of their homeland. Given that my father's family hailed from the region around Naples, where your *famiglia* determined your fate more than any other factor, the dissolution of his parents' marriage must have had an effect on my father, his sister, and the extended family.

My father stayed near Scranton with his father, who married a woman named Ruth a few years after the divorce. My father recalled his relationship with his stepmother as warm, if somewhat distant. By the time she came into his life, he was a teenager, so she was never really a maternal figure to him. He never discussed it with me, but I believe these early experiences had an impact in shaping his self-reliant and fiercely independent nature—and perhaps also on his decision to end his own first marriage when it was clear things weren't working out and to move on as amicably as possible.

The Carlucci family was well known in the Scranton area because of my great-grandfather's skill as a stonemason. Some of the buildings he worked on remain city landmarks, including several banks and churches, a county courthouse, a railroad station, and a post office. After arriving in Scranton in the mid-1880s, he began his own stone supply business, Carlucci & Bro., choosing a location close to the Delaware, Lackawanna & Western Railroad so materials from his quarries could be easily shipped around the country. The business was later renamed Carlucci Stone Co.[4] Interestingly, my great-grandfather was commissioned to construct the immigration station at Ellis Island, where he himself had passed through not long before. In an even more serendipitous turn of fate, he also was called upon to create the grand stairway at Arlington National Cemetery in Virginia. Little did he know his grandson would be buried there with full military honors after reaching one of the highest positions in the US government.

By the time my father was growing up, his family was well established in the community, and behaving respectably was no small matter. If young Frank disobeyed, he could expect to be spanked. At the dinner table, his father would use their notoriously long meals as an opportunity to grill him. It was not unusual for the "talk" to get quite intense—and for young Frank to leave the table fighting tears. My father's intense dislike for long dinners stayed with him for the rest of his life. He was often the first to finish, and the first ready to leave the table. Incidentally, he was also the first to arrive to the table, and most other places—he never wanted to be late for anything or keep anyone waiting.

My father lived near Bear Creek, where he would swim in the lake and explore the woods for hours. When he entered high school, he chose to attend Wyoming Seminary, a prep school in nearby Wilkes-Barre, Pennsylvania. He excelled academically and athletically and was proud to be accepted to Princeton University. Dad may have been compensating for his short stature of just over five feet (judicious reports later gave him a height of five feet seven), but there was not an exercise, sport, or competitive game he did not like—and he excelled in several. He was a star wrestler on both Wyoming Seminary and Princeton's wrestling teams and would later be initiated into the National Wrestling Hall of Fame. Princeton's football team treasured him because he could slip through, under, or around others in tight spots where no one else fit: a "little stick of dynamite."

All his life he biked, swam, and ran, and later in his life he played daily competitive tennis. It bothered me when my father would call me at college and ask: "How are your studies? Are you exercising?" Every time we spoke, I could expect these two questions. At the time I felt he was judging my choices and my weight. But now I know that what he was getting at was the idea of *mens sana in corpore sano*—the Latin phrase meaning "a healthy mind in a healthy body." He certainly believed in it in his own life.

He knew that it was up to him to make the most of his Princeton education, and he did. He met his longtime friend and future colleague Donald Rumsfeld there, along with others who would shape the direction of his life. He studied at the Woodrow Wilson School of Public and International Affairs (now the Princeton School of Public and International Affairs), which surely influenced his desire to enter the Foreign Service.

He also had a few adventures in his college years, including spending a summer in Mexico. My Aunt Joan liked to tell a story about him coming home and dumping out a suitcase full of used shoes—his idea of a good souvenir—on the living room floor. Frank II was none too happy about it. During his sophomore year, my father came home for Thanksgiving break in a used car he had just bought. He was very proud and couldn't wait to show it off.

His father quizzed him on all the details of his purchase, including whether he had insurance to drive it. Frank sheepishly said no. His father then demanded, "Get that car out of here right now!" That's how things often went between the two of them.

Another story from my father's college years sticks with me, as it speaks volumes about the type of man he was. Princeton has no fraternities or sororities, but instead has eating clubs that students in their junior year can apply to join. He got into a coveted club but one of his best friends didn't, so he turned down the membership and instead joined the club where his friend was accepted. His commitment to friendship was greater than his need for prestige. His loyalty, whether to a person or to a job he was tasked to perform, was a trait that held true throughout his life.

When he graduated from Princeton in 1952, my father joined the Naval Reserve Officer's Training Corps (NROTC) and went directly into the Navy. He was assigned as a first lieutenant on a destroyer escort based out of Seattle, where he was "basically the housekeeper," as he put it, making sure the ship was clean and painted. He also served as the gunnery and anti-submarine warfare (ASW) officer. He did not recall his Navy days particularly fondly:

> We spent a large number of days at sea serving as a training ship for Reserve forces. It was a rough riding ship, captained by a man who had no sense of seamanship. More significantly, he was a bully who would chew his officers out over the bullhorn. Each of us saved the ship at one time or another by actually countermanding his orders. While it wasn't the worst ship in the Navy, it was a long way from the best, and I was just as happy when my Navy tour came to an end.

One much retold story from this time—I never got it from my father but it was passed down through family lore—had to do with a depth charge (essentially an underwater explosive) being tested and going off a little shallowly, creating a small hole and a bit of a leak in the boat. As the gunnery officer, my father would have been at least partly responsible for conducting these tests. He did tell me that his ship's small size meant it was constantly bobbing up and down, especially in the rough waters around Alaska where they spent much of their time. The way he told me this made me think that perhaps he didn't have the stomach for seamanship. In fact, I don't ever recall seeing him on a boat by choice or for pleasure at any point in his life. Suffice it to say, my father was never really high on his career in the Navy—a bit ironic for a later secretary of defense.

Nonetheless, one significant event came from his years in the Navy. It was while he was on shore leave that he met his first wife, Jean Anthony. Jean and my father were married in Seattle and, once his tour of duty was over, they moved to Cambridge, Massachusetts. Frank dutifully attended Harvard Business School because of his father's wish that he become a businessperson. In a twist of fate, after in fact becoming a businessman himself later in life, my father would try to impart that same failed wisdom to me, which I would also suitably ignore. ("If you want to be successful, you need to study business or engineering in school," he used to tell me.) As soon as he had left the Navy, he began to be intrigued by the idea of a career in the Foreign Service. After one year at Harvard Business School, he left and moved to Washington, DC, to pursue the idea.

Though being a Foreign Service Officer (FSO) today is a different experience than it was in my father's day, some of the traits and motivations of those who feel called to foreign diplomacy remain the same. These include a sense of adventure, a fascination with other cultures, a desire to make a difference, and a belief in advancing American interests abroad.

An interesting look back at history shows us something that is hard to imagine today: when the Department of State was established by Congress in 1789, it consisted of about three staff members and translators. By the end of the eighteenth century, it had expanded to a not-so-robust ten staff members. At that time the United States only maintained diplomatic relations with France, Great Britain, the Netherlands, Portugal, and Spain, with partial representation to another half dozen countries. The Foreign Service remained relatively small until the end of World War II, after which there was a rapid increase in employees. Staffing levels doubled from around 1,650 immediately after the war to 3,436 by 1957. It was during this growth period that my father joined the Foreign Service.

The first step in the process of becoming an FSO is taking the Foreign Service written exam, which covers a gamut of topics including history, politics, culture, English, geography, economics, US government, math, and more. As anyone who has tried it knows, it is nearly impossible to prepare for this exam in any traditional way. You could be asked what Chinese dynasty followed the Ming in 1644 (it's the Qing) and then the next question could be "Which countries border Tanzania?" The State Department recommends reading a daily newspaper every day for a year to prepare for the exam.

In my father's day, the written exam was not much different and no less stressful. His memoirs record how nervous he was about the experience: "On the particular day when the written part of the service exam was given, I remember lying down flat in the car so I would not be spotted taking it by anyone, since I didn't want to jeopardize my current job if the exam didn't go well. Somehow, I got a passing grade."

When applicants pass the written component, they're invited to sit for the oral exam—a series of interviews and simulations that test decision-making skills and the ability to analyze complex scenarios. The test is only offered a few times a year and passing it is no small feat. Today about twenty thousand people take the test and only 2 to 3 percent pass, with even fewer joining the Foreign Service after undergoing the background check and receiving their first assignment.

After passing the exam and getting his security clearance, my father moved to Washington, DC, for the first time. Washington was the place he'd return to again and again over the course of his life. My father and his wife, Jean, moved to a "tiny steamy apartment in the Anacostia section of Washington," what was then a solidly middle-class neighborhood, inhabited mostly by mid-level government employees doing the work behind the scenes to support the lawmakers and headliners on Capitol Hill. The neighborhood suited my father just fine: he was a practical person who valued expediency and efficiency. As long as he could drive quickly and directly to where he needed to go, and provided there was a tennis court in the vicinity, he was fine. Anacostia is no longer a community where you'd find many bureaucrats. The neighborhood now has a crime rate 38 percent higher than in the rest of the District of Columbia, and per capita income is just over half of the per capita income for the rest of the city.[5]

Typically, an FSO's first assignment is to an office in the main State Department building or directly to an embassy abroad. Most

FSOs assigned directly to an embassy spend three months to a year in language training to prepare for their assignment. In 1956, my father was assigned to the Bureau of Near Eastern African and Asian Affairs. At the time this bureau covered North Africa, the Middle East, and parts of Asia. Today this office is known as the Bureau of Near Eastern Affairs (a bit of an odd way of referring to the Middle East) and largely covers the North African and Middle Eastern countries. Sub-Saharan Africa and East Asia are covered by separate offices.[6] According to my father's memoirs, his first assignment was "something called 'post management officer.' As post management officer, I became involved in the British attack on Egypt. My job was to keep track of the US personnel who were being evacuated."

My father described his initial role as "slightly above a file clerk." It doesn't sound very thrilling, but excitement did come along in the form of the Suez Crisis.[7] As foreign powers jockeyed for control of this critical piece of infrastructure, my father was helping to keep track of dependents of US citizens being evacuated.[8] He was then assigned to work on North Africa. This ping-ponging from different positions and geographical areas is fairly typical in the Foreign Service; you might go in with strong language skills or a preference toward working in one part of the world, but due to staffing needs you could be assigned to a completely different area where you have no background or experience.

But before he was assigned abroad, my father was lucky to land a position early on as an administrative assistant to outgoing ambassadors, thereby gaining access to higher levels of the State Department than a freshly minted FSO would normally have. He recounted:

> I also served as an Administrative Assistant to outgoing ambassadors, such as Ellsworth Bunker and Maxwell Gluck. Bunker sailed through Senate confirmation, but Gluck had an interesting exchange with Chairman Fulbright, the Chairman of the Foreign Affairs Committee. Gluck couldn't name the prime minister of the country to which he was being accredited.

Bunker was preparing for his appointment as ambassador to India. He had previously served as ambassador to Italy and to Argentina, and he would go on to become the ambassador to Vietnam. Gluck was the US ambassador to Ceylon (now Sri Lanka). Before becoming a political appointee, he founded and ran a chain of popular women's clothing stores and was a breeder of Thoroughbred horses. As my father recounted, Gluck famously couldn't recall the name of the premier of Ceylon when he was asked it in his confirmation hearing. Instead, Gluck responded by saying: "I look forward to learning that when I get to Colombo,"[9] thus becoming a bit of a poster child for those political appointees who are sometimes portrayed as better check-writers and party hosts than envoys.

At the time my father joined the Foreign Service, it was seen as an elite group comprised mostly of white men educated at East Coast universities. He noted that one of the things he did during his career was to "attempt to help the Foreign Service modernize itself. It was and is, to a certain extent even today, considered an elitist group with its own left-wing agenda." Women and minorities were rare in the service and were usually relegated to administrative positions. In recent years, especially in the last two decades, there has been a push to make our diplomatic corps more representative of the diversity of the United States. But until the early 1970s, the State Department expected women (but not men) in the Foreign Service to resign if they married, and women faced barriers in obtaining advanced language training and hardship posts, severely limiting both where they could be posted and their promotion opportunities.

Minorities were often limited to the "Negro Circuit" and the "Cucaracha Circuit"—insensitive "euphemisms" for the State Department's practice of assigning Black FSOs only to Africa and the Caribbean and Hispanic FSOs to Latin America. Overt sexism and racism did not improve much until the Foreign Service Act of 1980 explicitly prohibited these practices.[10]

My father wanted to be appointed to Latin America, and his subsequent excitement about an appointment to Africa was somewhat unique for the time, especially when many diplomats sought cushier assignments in Europe.

Generally, the path to promotions, as evidenced by some of my father's difficult early appointments, is paved with hardship posts and unglamorous grunt work. Frank was itching to get out into the field. My father's time as a desk jockey would soon come to an end.

CHAPTER TWO

AFRICAN ADVENTURES

MY FATHER WAS BRIEFLY disappointed when he wasn't assigned to Latin America for his first post overseas. He instead found himself on his way to South Africa in 1957. As was typical, once he had his mandate—whether he liked it or not—he did not complain or shirk from the work required. He noted, "South Africa, in particular Cape Town, where we landed, was a beautiful place. We found an apartment, reasonably close to the US consulate, and it was there in my free time that I started to hit some tennis balls. The climate was ideal, and a lot of the South Africans had tennis courts in their backyards. Thus began a lifelong avocation for me."

His official job title was economic commercial reporting officer at the US consulate in Johannesburg. One of his duties was researching and writing the *Basic Annual Industries Report*, which assessed the state and performance of the key industries in South

Africa. US companies used these reports to assess opportunities for investments in South Africa. This type of commercial diplomacy isn't as well known to those outside the Foreign Service as government-to-government diplomacy, but it's an essential function of embassies and consulates in their goal to promote US business abroad.

As he learned more about the place, he remarked:

> South Africa seemed to have every resource except oil, which they made from coal. The real challenge for the country was racial harmony. While South Africa was a great place to live, there was a shadow hanging over it. Racial tensions were becoming more threatening. I did not think South Africa was going to be able to make the transition. I, quite frankly, thought South Africa would explode someday, but thanks to God and [Nelson] Mandela, I was proved wrong.

In South Africa he dove headlong into learning the history of the African continent and became especially fascinated with the anti-apartheid movement.

> I began to follow political activities on my own time. I went to meetings of the African National Congress (ANC) and got my picture taken by the "Special Branch," a much-feared police unit of the South African Government, but I persisted. Our ambassador got called into the Foreign Ministry and was asked about my activities and the response was that since my tour end was coming up anyway, they shouldn't make a fuss about it.

My father started attending ANC meetings on his own initiative. Since 1948 the central purpose of the ANC had been to oppose apartheid, and it was still leading the charge for that movement. For official reasons, the US embassy could not be seen attending or endorsing these meetings due to their clandestine nature. As his notes above relate, my father's activities were noticed by the "Special Branch" police unit of the South African government and eventually the ambassador at the time, Henry A. Byroade (ambassador to South Africa from 1956 to 1959).[11] What he was doing wasn't illegal, but it ran the risk of offending the host government.

The founding ideology of the ANC was voting equality among all South Africans, Black and white. At the time, white South Africans controlled the government and possessed most of the wealth in the country, despite comprising less than 20 percent of the population.[12] The ANC began as a legitimate party but became known as a militant party following the Sharpeville massacre in 1960.[13] The massacre, one of the largest in South African history, was organized by an offshoot of the ANC, the Pan-Africanist Congress (PAC), and resulted in the death of sixty-nine people at (what was allegedly) a peaceful protest outside of a police station. They were protesting what was known as the Pass Law, which required all Black South Africans to carry a passbook to identify themselves at all times (the white South Africans were exempt).[14]

My father was one of the first Americans to talk to Robert Sobukwe, who founded the PAC, during his rise in prominence and before his arrest in 1960 following the Sharpeville massacre. My father specifically mentions him in a Foreign Service dispatch to the State Department in 1959: "Although Sobukwe himself is undoubtedly sincere, he will probably find it a difficult task to control some of the more extremist Africans under him."[15] The ANC, too, became increasingly militant, engaging in guerrilla warfare and sabotage from 1960 to 1964 when many of the ANC leaders were arrested and thrown in prison (including Nelson Mandela). The ANC was made illegal by the white South African government from 1960 to 1990 and operated in secrecy as an underground movement until it was legalized in 1990. Nelson Mandela became the head of the party and won the election in 1994, forming a multiracial government and bringing an end to apartheid. The ANC has been the ruling party in South Africa since 1994, having won every election since then, despite recent controversies leading to low levels of support.

My father was on the ground in South Africa during a critical few years. He was listening to ANC meetings just before they were driven underground and likely saw the buildup in tensions that led to Sharpeville. He interacted with some of the key figures of the anti-apartheid movement before they were imprisoned, including Sobukwe, who was to South Africa what Malcolm X was to America.

In an interview, my father recalled that there were no Black Americans posted to South Africa at this time. The intention was likely to prevent confusion and to avoid agitating the apartheid government of South Africa, but this wasn't an official policy. He went on to say:

> The guidance that I had was that apartheid was wrong, we didn't favor it. And we were certainly in those days much less activist in opposing that kind of poor human rights policy. But it was clear that we did not favor it. When I'd see lines that said "Europeans only," I was frequently tempted

> to get into the other line and say I was not a European. I certainly found the segregation distasteful. And I must say I found a number of South Africans who felt the same way.[16]

At the time, the United States didn't agitate for human rights in South Africa and simply recognized the apartheid government as legitimate. It's only in hindsight that we see more clearly how truly awful it was: or at least, that's what we can tell ourselves.

My half sister, Karen, my father's first child, was born during this time. He never spoke to me directly about becoming a father or its impact on him—in keeping with his tendency to keep his emotions and feelings about personal events of consequence close to the vest. We always knew that he cared deeply about his family, and he showed that to us in many ways. Outward displays of emotion were not one of them, nor were heartfelt or soul-searching conversations.

After South Africa, my father was off to a more dangerous destination—the Congo. As he wrote in his memoirs:

> The fact that I had engaged in political reporting on a volunteer basis must have caught the attention of somebody in the State Department because my next assignment was indeed challenging. I was sent to Leopoldville (as it was called in those days), the capital of the Democratic Republic

of the Congo. I arrived just fifteen days before independence in June 1960. I rented a car and rapidly assumed the role of the outrider of the embassy. I would go around from event to event—Prime Minister Patrice Lumumba governed by press conference—in order to monitor the situation.

It's tempting to speculate whether my father was sent to the Congo because he was already seen as something of a live wire and it was an easy way to keep him far afield, or because he'd shown skill at dealing with fraught social situations. What's not open for question is that the Congo was on the brink of catastrophe when he arrived.

The Congo is a complex place with a long and difficult history. In 1885 Belgian King Leopold II acquired land rights to the Congo territory, naming it the Congo Free State (1887–1908).[17] The Congo Free State became notorious for its brutal treatment of the Congolese. Beatings and forced labor were used to turn all inhabitants into slave workers for one of history's most widely reviled kings. Colonists drained the country of natural resources, chiefly rubber, palm oil, ivory, and minerals. The *Force Publique* emerged at this time as a group of African soldiers under European officers who enforced Leopold's will. *Force Publique* soldiers would cut off the hands of dissenters, including children, and show them as proof of subjugation. Failure to meet mining or harvesting quotas was punishable by death. The population of the Congo was decimated from over twenty million to between eight and ten million in only twenty years. This was one of the worst genocides in history—and arguably the worst case of colonial abuse in history.

When word got out about the atrocities committed in the Congo, the Belgian parliament stepped in and took over the administration of the Congo from King Leopold, reconstituting the colony as the Belgian Congo (1908–1960).[18] The Congolese were still mistreated and exploited, forced into indentured servitude as European investors established plantations and mines. Belgium portrayed its relationship with the Congo as one of a parent and a child, a view that continued until the 1950s. France and the United Kingdom began to release their colonies in the 1950s, and the pressure was growing externally and internally (in the form of rising nationalist movements and demonstrations) for Belgium to follow suit. ABAKO (*Alliance des Bakongo*), a Bakongo cultural association for Bantu-speaking people from the Congo, emerged in 1950. ABAKO became a leading group in nationalist, anticolonial sentiment that quickly spread throughout the country. The first Congolese political party, the Congo National Movement (*Mouvement National Congolais*, MNC), was created in 1958 by Patrice Lumumba and others.

In January 1959, about a year and a half before my father arrived there, anti-European riots broke out in Leopoldville (now Kinshasa). Violent altercations continued between Belgian forces and Congolese militants from 1959 to 1960. Belgium had maintained that independence for the Congo would not be possible anytime soon, with unofficial plans for a thirty-year transition period. Facing violence and losing control of the situation, Belgium suddenly ceded and began making arrangements for the Congo's independence. This was extremely reactionary and did not provide the time or resources for a successful handoff of power to the Congolese government, which didn't even exist yet. Overnight, on June 30, 1960, the Congo became an experiment in instantaneous independence, resulting in chaos and panic. Several provinces within the country made unsuccessful secessionist attempts soon after independence. The country would be renamed the Republic of Zaire in 1971 and then the Democratic Republic of the Congo, its name from 1997 to the present.

In his memoirs, my father described the atmosphere and the concerns of the US Foreign Service in the weeks leading up to the Congolese independence:

> I arrived fifteen days before independence. We had a Consul General who was leaving, and an ambassador had been designated, Clare Timberlake. The situation was one of considerable confusion. Nobody knew what was going to happen on the day of independence. There was a lot of focus in the consulate general on getting our independence delegation in place, making sure we were appropriately represented. There was a feeling that we did not really know the real African leadership. What was it going to be? Who was it going to be? What did the Belgians let go of at the time of independence? There were just a lot of unanswered questions. Some felt the Belgians had gone too fast. Everybody knew that education-wise the Congolese were not fully prepared for independence so there was anticipation of difficulty.

As a colonial power, the Belgians trained no civil service, did not allow the Congolese to self-govern, and did not organize any higher education programs. They concentrated instead on turning out medical orderlies, mechanics, and clerks. Only 3,500 of the sixteen thousand primary schools in the country provided secondary schooling at the time. Nearly 70 percent of children left school before completing four years, and literacy rates were low. At the time of independence in 1960, there were only sixteen Congolese college graduates in the entire country.

The Belgian policy was aptly labeled "paternalism" by both its advocates and its detractors. Had decolonization proceeded at an unhurried pace, the Congo may have emerged prepared for democratic self-rule. This is not to say, of course, that this inevitably would have occurred, but the country would have had a far better chance of building from the basic foundation of educational infrastructure that the Belgians created. In any case, decolonization happened very rapidly, and the Congo emerged from colonial rule with a relatively complex political, economic, and financial system, and virtually no Congolese prepared to lead it. To make matters worse, the Congolese economy was also in poor health at the time of independence: the country's gold and foreign exchange reserves were deteriorating, and there had been a sharp increase in urban unemployment. This was the situation when my father arrived, and it only got worse from there. He recalled:

> I persuaded the DCM [deputy chief of mission], Rob McIlvaine, a marvelous man, to allow me to rent a Volkswagen so I had my own car and didn't go around in an embassy chauffeured car. I then got myself some press credentials because the press moved around more freely than anybody else could. Lumumba tended to hold a press conference a day and I figured it was important to get into those. Then I got myself a pass to the Parliament which was in formation.

My father was keeping up his reputation as a "maverick" FSO. He was practicing diplomacy—but not in quite the way he was taught at the Foreign Service Institute. Instead, my father was adept at reading the situation on the ground and assessing who he needed to get to know and how. As he described it: "I'd sit in the bar in the Parliament and go up and shake hands with them and strike up a conversation. I got to know Patrice Lumumba under fairly adverse circumstances . . . I basically spent all day outside the embassy. Just floating in from time to time."[19]

His unorthodox approach allowed him to get the lay of the land and get close to the leadership of the country very quickly. That's not to say that he fit in, exactly—certainly not among Africans and not really among envoys either. Reporters quipped that as "a blue-eyed man with a crew cut, Carlucci hardly fits the popular image of a diplomat. He looks as if he would be more at home coaching a high school baseball team than representing this nation in delicate diplomatic dealings in Africa."[20] The article went on to say that "his youth and athletic energy have been assets on posts where courage and physical agility have sometimes counted as much as statesmanship." Perhaps all the wrestling he had done on the mat in high school and college had unforeseen payoffs in a very different arena.

My father recalled the events immediately following the Congolese independence:

> Independence in June of 1960 had led to chaos. I can recall our houseboy asking me, "Boss, when will independence end?" The entire residential area where I lived, called Djelo Binza, was evacuated. As I drove around, I could even hear phonographs that people had not turned off in their haste to leave. As we drove down the mountain, we were stopped by a soldier who talked to us while he

waved a bayonet in the face of my five-year-old daughter, Karen. I can remember throwing the wife of the General Service Officer, who was pregnant, onto an escape barge just as it was pulling away. Jean and Karen went to Ghana for safety, where they stayed about a month.

Parliamentary elections had resulted in a huge victory for the MNC, led by Patrice Lumumba, making him the first prime minister. The parliament elected Joseph Kasavubu from ABAKO as president. The two had an uneasy partnership; neither had earned enough votes to form an outright majority. A senate and assembly were installed at the national and regional level.

The *Force Publique* was the military of the Congo and remained the formal power in society despite being largely led by white Europeans, who retained their power temporarily until suitable Black replacements could be found (and unfortunately there were no suitable replacements due to poor education of the native population after decades of subjugation). As my father noted, there was a lot of confusion about the future of the Congo at this time. This vestige of colonial power became a powder keg. "The panic with which the Belgians fled was amazing. I went around my neighborhood, and remember a houseboy coming out and telling me his employer had said, 'Take everything; it's all yours.' People fled literally in their nightgowns. The neighborhoods were deserted for quite some time."

My father was often mistaken for a Belgian (i.e., public enemy No. 1) in the ensuing chaos. White officers and civilians were attacked, white-owned properties were looted, and white women were raped. White civilians fled to neighboring countries as refugees. This came as a huge shock to the world—Belgium had portrayed its colony of the Congo as an idyllic society of coexistence between the Black and white populations. To see the country devolve into anarchy and violence immediately after its independence created international outrage and prompted a response from the Belgian government.[21]

The United States was interested in the Congo (along with the other newly created countries following the global wave of decolonization) as proxy states for the Cold War with the Soviet Union. At the time, the Cold War was fought by bringing in neutral countries either to capitalism or communism in a competition for spheres of influence. The Cuban Missile Crisis would happen in 1962, less than two years after the Congo crisis, showing how close the two sides were to active conflict. The Congo crisis was a key Cold War event. Reports from Lawrence Devlin, the CIA chief of station in Leopoldville (Kinshasa), described the situation in the Congo as a textbook Communist takeover.[22]

Some of my father's memories from this time were particularly vivid:

> I remember one day a soldier approached the US Embassy and started waving his rifle as if to shoot. With the ambassador's permission, I went out and confronted him using an embassy driver to convert my French into Lingala. The soldier said, "You have Belgians in there and I want them!"
>
> I said, "There are no Belgians. But look at this flag, this is the American flag, and you have no right to point the rifle at us. It's your job to protect us!" To my surprise, he agreed and accompanied me to a nearby hotel where some Americans were being held as hostages. He persuaded his colleagues to let the Americans go. I had found a new friend!

> On the day of independence, I had heard rumors that rioting was occurring at the parliament building so I [went out and] asked what they were rioting about. The answer was interesting. They were upset not so much at the Belgians as at their own leadership, Patrice Lumumba and others, who had suddenly sprouted big cars, big houses, and flashy suits . . . They asked, "What's in it for us? Everybody else gets something and we get nothing." Subsequently, Lumumba, who was an absolute spellbinder, a very charismatic man . . . went out to the military camp at Djelo Binza and talked to the soldiers. He managed to turn them against the Belgians. That's when anti-Belgian rioting started.

On July 5, a week after independence, Black Congolese soldiers in the *Force Publique* mutinied against their white Belgian commanders at the Thysville military base. The mutiny quickly spread to other bases and violence broke out across the country.

> When chaos broke loose . . . Ralph Bunche [the under secretary for political affairs] . . . came out [to visit the Congo] just after independence. Prior to that, we had been through the evacuation, the rapes, and the pillaging. We were living in the embassy around the clock. He dictated a cable calling on the UN to send in a multinational force from my office. I was standing right beside him when he dictated the cable.

My father was holed up in the US embassy, which was positioned at the edge of the capital city on the banks of the Congo River.

Right now, though, the situation in the Congo commanded his full attention and that of the world's major superpowers as well. The Belgians brought in troops to restore order and to protect their citizens without seeking permission from Lumumba. On July 9, Belgian paratroopers landed in the Congo, ostensibly to protect fleeing Belgian citizens. The Congolese government promptly went to the UN to demand the removal of Belgian troops, and the UN agreed. The United States supported this UN effort.

As my father recalled:

> [UN] Peacekeeping has a somewhat mixed reputation these days, but the Congo has to be characterized as a very successful multinational peacekeeping operation. The troops who came in—the Ghanaians, the Moroccans, the Nigerians, Ethiopians, subsequently Indians, Pakistanis—all did a marvelous job.
>
> I went out to the airport and spent the day acting like [an air traffic] controller, an airline attendant, and what have you . . . But we got the [UN] airplanes in. Meanwhile the Belgian troops had moved in to take over part of the airport.
>
> Towards the end of the day, Rob McIlvaine, the DCM, called me and said, "Patrice Lumumba called and wants to go to Stanleyville and would we take him." . . . I guess that was early afternoon. Well, he didn't show up until about 5:00 and just drove out onto the tarmac with a big entourage. On the other side, the Belgian forces drove up and confronted him. I was standing in the middle between the two forces with machine guns pointed at each other.

Lumumba said, "I'm here to go to Stanleyville and you're going to take me."

The aircraft commander came up and said, "We've just learned that the controllers in Stanleyville have been killed and all the lights are out. We're not going."

The Belgian colonel said, "Unless you get these people off the tarmac in five minutes, I'm opening fire." So, I had a dilemma on my hands.

I finally grabbed the aircraft commander and I said, "I don't care if we fly up to Stanleyville, turn around, and fly back. We're getting in this airplane right now or there is going to be gunfire here."

He said, "Okay." So, I took Lumumba and [Joseph] Kasavubu both to Stanleyville.

Stanleyville, now known as Kisangani, was the political central base of the MNC and a stronghold of Lumumba's. Despite being somewhat rootless overall in terms of an allegiance to a particular province or locale, Lumumba felt an allegiance to the city thanks to the fact that he had once been employed as a clerk at Stanleyville's central post office.

Lumumba was prime minister and Kasavubu was president at that point. I told him that we had a problem in Stanleyville, but if they insisted on going, I would take them. They said we insist on going. In fact, Lumumba had screamed at me. He called me and he said something to the effect that "You Europeans are all hypocrites. You promised me."

And when we got on the airplane, I said, "Why did you scream at me?"

He said, "I didn't realize you were an American. I thought you were European." They stood in the cockpit the entire flight to Stanleyville. On the way up, I told them that there were Europeans in Stanleyville, and I assumed they didn't have any objection if we took them back on the plane. Lumumba agreed.

Then when we got off the plane, the Europeans [in Stanleyville] came to me and said, "We want to leave but the immigration authorities won't let us leave."

I said, "Well, I'm not your consul but I'll see what I can do." So, I went around to the governor's house in Stanleyville where Lumumba and Kasavubu were having a cocktail party and talked to Lumumba and said, "We have done you a favor by bringing you up here . . . You should let these people loose."

And he responded with something like, "These are bad 'Flemish,' and they shouldn't be allowed to go." But then he turned to me—he was tall, and I am short—and dropped his hand on my shoulder and said, "But I like you. You are my friend. I give you the Belgians. It's a gift."

I said, "Don't give it as a gift, but I'm happy to take them." For several years, I received Christmas cards and other messages from the Belgians for "saving their lives."

The Congo was the focus of world attention. It was at the heart of the Cold War struggle at the time. There was a lot of feeling that Lumumba was a communist sympathizer. We had Senator Dodd, Tom Dodd [senator from Connecticut from 1959 to 1971 and father of Chris Dodd, who

> would go on to be senator from Connecticut from 1981 to 2011], who was an active critic of people like Lumumba and Gbenye, the latter being Lumumba's interior minister. Dodd came out and I was his escort officer. I thought he had become convinced that Lumumba and Gbenye, while they may have had some sympathy for the Soviets, didn't really understand what communism was. But when he went back to the US, he called them communists again.

Lumumba's outreach to the Soviet Union at the peak of the crisis resulted in the arrival of technicians and matériel from Soviet Bloc countries. This convinced members of the US leadership at the time that Lumumba had to be removed. CIA Director Dulles noted, "Lumumba is an opportunist and not a Communist. His final decision to which camp he will belong will not be made by him but rather will be imposed upon him by outside forces."[23] The United States quickly devised a plan to unseat Lumumba and to assassinate him if necessary.

Soon after the Congo itself gained independence, the wealthy Katanga province declared its independence from the new country, followed by the South Kasai province in August. The nascent Congolese government was at an impasse regarding how to respond to this breakup. Tensions were already high between Lumumba and Kasavubu due to the violence, international attention on the Congo, and their differing opinions on the presence of UN peacekeepers. Lumumba insisted that force be used to bring back the Katanga region into the state, even making this case when he visited the White House. Kasavubu strongly resented this idea. Tensions were ratcheting up even higher, and the country felt like a powder keg. My father quite literally felt this firsthand.

A few months [after the flight to Stanleyville], I was on my way to the airport to meet visiting Deputy Secretary of State Loy Henderson. I was traveling in a car driven by the embassy warrant officer. Inside, in addition to me, were our defense attaché and his wife. The driver was going very fast in spite of my repeated requests for him to slow down. Tragedy happened. We hit a bicyclist crossing the road and he was thrown off and killed. Our car went into a ditch. In those days, when there were fatal car-pedestrian accidents, crowds frequently murdered the driver. I shouted at the driver to get away from the car. The defense attaché couldn't get out because his wife was in shock. I did the only possible thing. I went over to the body to draw a rapidly gathering crowd away from the car. Two separate embassy employees attempted to help me but couldn't get to me.

Then the crowd started beating me up. I felt what I thought was a hard blow to my back, and about that time—actually somebody else, I think Lawrence "Larry" Devlin stopped as well—and shouted at me and said, "Some people will take you into the village."

I said, "Larry, the last place I want to go is into the village."

It was getting fairly serious when a Congolese bus driver drove his bus right through the crowd and opened his door right at my back and I just stepped into the bus. I didn't know I had been stabbed until I saw the pool of blood on the floor of the bus. He, in essence, saved my life. I was taken to the hospital where I received seven or eight stitches in my back and in my head.

The remaining six months in the Congo were just as exciting as the first six. Lumumba would single me out in press conferences and was decidedly friendly; not so his speeches, which were nationalistic with an anti-Western tone. Some thought he was a Communist, but I doubt he understood what communism was. He did understand there were two sides in the Cold War, and he could play one against the other. We shared his vision of a united Congo, but the US government could not deal with his erratic behavior.

When it became clear that Lumumba was amassing power, the Congolese military moved and put him under house arrest. He went into his residence, and it was only when he left his residence to try to flee that he was captured. Had he stayed in his residence, he probably wouldn't have been captured. As it was, myself and then Senator Gale McGee were probably the last two Westerners to see him alive. We were having a drink about mid-afternoon at a sidewalk café and a truck went by. Lumumba had his hands tied behind his back and was in the rear part of the truck. The truck was on the way to the airport. As you know, he was killed either in the airplane or shortly after he got off the airplane in the Katanga.

The historical backdrop to my father's notes about the transfer of power in the Congo and the death of Lumumba include the following events: On September 5, 1960, Kasavubu relieved Lumumba of his functions, and Lumumba responded by dismissing Kasavubu, creating two governments within the Congo. Colonel Joseph Mobutu of the Congolese National Army (ANC) stepped in and orchestrated a coup d'état on September 14 and ordered the Soviets out of the country. Lumumba was arrested in December and killed in January of 1961.

Lumumba was blamed for a plot to arrest Mobutu, and this led to his arrest by Katangan forces. These Belgian-led Katangan troops likely were the ones who killed Lumumba on January 17, 1961. At the time, my father was in Stanleyville; he was going back and forth between Stanleyville and the US embassy in Leopoldville, the most important inland city and major port at the time, to act as consul. On the radio it was announced that Lumumba had been murdered by a "paratroop colonel" named Carlucci. Even an official cable to UN Secretary-General Dag Hammarskjöld reported my father had killed Lumumba!

To this day it's unclear who exactly killed Lumumba; it was most likely a Belgian or American operative. My father hitchhiked out of Stanleyville on a UN plane to Bukavu and then to Elizabethville, then back to Leopoldville. He went back to Stanleyville a few weeks later and was put under house arrest and declared a persona non grata.[24] This stripped him of his diplomatic immunity and is generally a method for a host country to expel a diplomat they no longer wish to deal with.

In 2000 a French movie erroneously covered my father's involvement in Lumumba's assassination, putting him at a clandestine meeting . . . and my father stood up in the theater and said as much.

> I spoke to the audience after the film had been shown and told them that I was never at any such meeting, the scene was false. I threatened to sue, even though my lawyer said my chances of winning were slim because I was a public figure. Nevertheless, the threat worked, and the film company then bleeped out that portion of the film.

He did not like how the film suggested the degree of his involvement in or knowledge about the killing of Lumumba. He also took issue with how sweaty and winded the character playing him appeared on screen. "I was never as fat as that guy!" he also reportedly added to his post-screening speech.

My father's exploits in the Congo are somewhat legendary within the Foreign Service. He was boldly moving around at a time when chaos was rampant, and he was the point man interacting with all of the top figures in Congolese politics. At this time there was a disconnect between Washington and overseas posts. He seems to have flourished in that environment and operated extremely effectively on his loose leash. Today, these sorts of exploits would be impossible and FSOs are much more closely monitored.

After my father returned to the United States, Cyrille Adoula, one of the Congolese leaders whom he had befriended, came to Washington, which resulted in an interesting episode that was later mentioned in the *New York Times*. My father's notes about it are as follows:

> Adoula visited the US, and I was the escort officer. A lunch was arranged at the White House. I was at Blair House shuffling suitcases when Adoula sat down at the lunch, looked around the table and asked President Kennedy, "Où est Carlucci? (Where is Carlucci?)"
>
> "Who the hell is Carlucci?" Kennedy asked. Word was passed down and finally reached Assistant Secretary of State for African Affairs G. Mennen "Soapy" Williams, who had me summoned to the White House. As I walked in, Angie Biddle Duke, chief of protocol, welcomed me.

"What am I doing here?" I asked.

"I don't know," Duke replied, "but there's an empty chair over there. Go sit down."

About that time Soapy Williams tapped me on the shoulder and said "Frank, the interpreter for the president has not shown up. Go up and interpret."

The president, through me, turned not to his right but to his left and asked the governor of the National Bank of the Congo, Albert Ndele, what the economic situation was like in the Congo. With that, Ndele took off like a rocket, throwing out all kinds of figures on gross national product, foreign exchange, and Lord knows what else. I was trying to convert the francs into dollars at the rate of 60 francs per dollar. I will never forget it. After what seemed an eternity, he stopped. He looked at me. The president looked at me.

"Well, what did he say?" the president finally asked. I looked at my notes and could make nothing out of them.

"Mr. President, he says the economic situation in the Congo is not very good right now." With that, the president tried his French, and my interpreting career came to an abrupt end. I didn't interpret again for a high official until I interpreted for President Ronald Reagan when Prime Minister Mário Soares visited Washington, DC.

The *New York Times* described the Kennedy incident this way:

Mr. Carlucci, who served fifteen years as a Foreign Service Officer and distinguished himself in Africa, once befriended Cyrille Adoula, who later became the premier of the Congo.

> At a state luncheon in the White House in 1962, Mr. Adoula asked, "Where's Carlucci?"
>
> The cry went down from President Kennedy to Secretary of State Dean Rusk to lesser lights, "Who's Carlucci?" He was found eating lunch across the street with other junior staff members and rushed to the state dining room in time to provide a happy ending to just one in a series of escapades that marked his State Department career.[25]

The UN remained in the Congo to stabilize the country as a handful of technocrats attempted to govern. After this failed, Mobutu launched a second coup (with the backing of the military), taking over the country as a dictator. He had the backing of the United States as well, who saw him as a stable, pro-Western partner they could work with. Mobutu would remain in power for over thirty years, through 1997, when another military coup unseated him and sent him into exile, where he died from cancer just three months later. During his time as leader, Mobutu oversaw widespread corruption and embezzlement, and was notorious for taking extravagant trips while his country experienced economic stagnation.

In 1962 the State Department gave my father The Superior Service Award for his actions in the Congo. He experienced more action in his first two tours than many diplomats would in their entire careers. And he was just getting started.

CHAPTER THREE

AROUND *the* WORLD

AFTER A FEW EXCITING and exhausting years in Africa, in late 1961 my father asked to return home to the States to be closer to his father, who was in ill health. My father's relationship with his father had evolved from one of uneasy circumspection to one of mutual respect. From there it morphed further into what I would call begrudging admiration. My grandfather was never overt in his praise of my father, but as my father's career developed, it was clear that Frank II was proud of his son's success. True to family form, Frank II was glad to give glowing quotes about his son in interviews with newspaper reporters but highly unlikely to say positive things to my father's face. Still, the sentiment was there.

It was a challenge for my father to come back to Washington and play the part of a desk jockey again. His official title was officer in charge of Congolese affairs. One positive aspect of the work was the chance to work with a few people my father admired, including

Ambassadors G. McMurtrie "Mac" Godley and Edmund "Ed" Gullion. Another was the fact that the Congo remained a topic of keen international focus; President Kennedy himself took a personal interest in the country. It was therefore not uncommon for my father and his colleagues to be summoned to the White House for a quick briefing. Dad was part of a coalition that took a strong position in favor of a unified Congo. He recalled:

> Whenever we got into real trouble, we would use Ed Gullion, who was then the ambassador [to the Congo]. Kennedy liked Ed Gullion. He'd met him in Vietnam or someplace and liked him personally. Gullion was a marvelous man, very bright, very articulate. So, when we felt ourselves sliding down the slope, we'd call Gullion back for consultation and have him go over and see the president. And that always worked. Kennedy's instincts were quite good.

The Katanga province still sought to break away from the rest of the country of Congo and become independent, a controversial and divisive subject. Some thought that if one province went, others would also splinter off, leaving the area increasingly vulnerable to the continued Soviet influence and presence in the region. Others thought that the cost of intervening was too high, and that the country should be left to its own devices. My father was on the side of those who thought the province should be brought back into the fold, while "[t]he European bureau tended to sympathize with the Katanga secessionists, and George McGee, who was under secretary of state, frankly, would vacillate on the issue." My father recalled that he and his team were committed to their position and were quite hard charging.

In 1963 my father left the Congo Desk for a brief tour in Personnel. It was less hectic but not nearly challenging enough. The only way he could stomach this desk job was with the knowledge that it was only temporary—and he did later acknowledge that he appreciated that he had a stable Washington posting in time for my half brother Chip's birth.

Frank "Chip" Carlucci IV was born on February 25, 1963, in Washington, DC. At the time, the family of four had moved into a small home on Albemarle Street in northwest Washington. I can only assume that when my father found out he was having a boy, the baby's name was set in stone—he would be the fourth Frank Charles Carlucci. It was a pretty grand name for a young boy to live up to. At the time, Frank II and Frank III were still very much alive, and his mother liked the nickname "Chip" for my brother because it helped to avoid confusion. My brother was never fond of the moniker, and to this day it's a family name only.

My father's next overseas assignment came in early 1964, when he was assigned to Zanzibar. The tiny island had become a focal point of the Cold War. Newly independent from the British, the unrest there boiled over into a massacre of the ruling Arabs who were associated with the Brits. The country's contacts with China and the USSR greatly expanded and Western ambassadors were kicked out.

Averell Harriman, who was under secretary of state, gave my father essentially two instructions: get a NASA tracking station on the island back into operation, and make sure that Zanzibar did not become a global flashpoint and a political embarrassment to President Lyndon B. Johnson during the upcoming presidential campaign.[26]

The '60s were a tumultuous time in much of the world, and

this was certainly true on the forty-two-by-thirty-five-mile main island of Zanzibar. The small island chain off the east coast of Tanzania in the Indian Ocean has long had an outsized historical and economic importance as a crossroads for trade between the Middle East and mainland Africa, and since the 1500s, with Europe as well. This gave the country an uncommon cultural complexity and diversity. When my father arrived, the island was newly self-governing after Britain ended its status as a protectorate on December 10, 1963. In January 1964, a revolution led to the rise of Communist-trained leader John Okello, who was hugely popular within the country. He gave passionate speeches full of fiery rhetoric that encouraged the oppressed ethnic African majority to rise up and overthrow the Arabic minority that had long held sway over the island. The resulting coup and ensuing violence led to the murder of two thousand to four thousand people. Many more, especially Arabs and Indians, fled the archipelago. An African-led Socialist government came into power, much to the dismay of the West. It wasn't led by Okello, however, who came to be seen as too much of a live wire. Instead, in January 1964, Abeid Amani Karume became Zanzibar's first president.

Karume and other African leaders in Zanzibar quickly expanded their contacts with the USSR and China. Zanzibar was being referred to as the "Cuba of Africa." The 1962 Cuban Missile Crisis was fresh in everyone's minds, and now came the potential for another standoff between the United States and Soviet Union. The US consul, Fritz Picard, was marched out of the country, literally at gunpoint. Only a handful of Americans were left by the time my father arrived in Zanzibar.

Shortly before he got there, the local stadium in Stone Town was renamed the Mao Tse Tung Stadium and the island's main hospital became the V. I. Lenin Hospital. The British Club became the People's Club, of which my father was a fan because it meant access to a tennis court and free tennis balls and ball boys. Of course he related global geopolitical machinations to his ability to get time on a tennis court . . .

My father described the foreign presence in Zanzibar:

> The Soviets and the Chinese flooded the place. There were well over one hundred Soviets attached to their embassy and the East Germans had a very significant presence. . . We had a North Vietnamese embassy. We had a North Korean embassy and a very substantial Chinese Communist presence, hardly matched by a very small British and American presence. I think there were three of us, a vice consul, one other officer, and a secretary or two . . . A very small British presence and that was it as far as the West was concerned.[27]

Establishing even this very small Western presence was no small feat. Lengthy negotiations went into reopening the US consulate and turning it into an embassy. At the time, the top brass at the State Department wanted to let the British take the lead and the United States to play a secondary role, but my father and others thought we should have a more robust presence on the island.

My father repeatedly went to Dar es Salaam to work on the issue with then Ambassador William "Bill" Leonhart. These trips to mainland Tanzania (then Tanganyika) were always an ordeal, as he had to fly in an aging 1930s de Havilland aircraft that could only hold about four or five people at once. The pilot had a habit of pulling out a novel to read the minute the wheels got off the ground, which my father found a bit disconcerting. Eventually, Zanzibari President Abeid Amani Karume agreed that the United States could reopen our diplomatic post on the island.

My father spent the first year in Zanzibar as one of the few US representatives in the country and saw it as part of his job to help spread Western influence. He would meet with the president, observe political events, and report back to the State Department. In his recollections, he noted that there were no major victories for the West, and he felt he made little progress, but he did grow friendly with British and Israeli counterparts and even befriended the Soviet ambassador, who gave him a small Russian doll for my half sister Karen.

There were very few Americans in the country at the time, and the US did not formally recognize the Vietnamese, North Korean, or East German governments, meaning that at formal functions my father couldn't interact with their representatives. Instead, he focused on developing a relationship with President Karume. Karume himself wasn't a devout communist and had some goodwill toward the West. When my father asked Karume what my father could do to improve Western relations with Zanzibar, Karume told him to learn Swahili. Another incident my father recalled further cemented that this would be a good idea:

> In one of the more humorous incidents, I decided to visit the neighboring island of Pemba, which was being run by a commissar (an official of the Communist Party) named Ali Sultan Issa, a man who was trained in Beijing. He was so indoctrinated that he insisted we even share the same bed. "This is the way we do it in the People's democracy." He took me around the island with people chanting and

> singing since it was a "workers' paradise." Then he had a rally, and during the rally . . . he would point at me, and the crowd would applaud and yell and scream. So, I asked someone what he was saying. He told me he was saying, "There's the enemy. Applaud if you think we ought to throw the Americans out!" Right then and there, I decided that learning Swahili was essential.

My father's knack for languages allowed him to pick up Swahili quickly, and he used it to great effect in creating a rapport with what could have been a natural enemy. Some months later at a cocktail party, my father greeted President Karume in his own language. The Soviet ambassador then came up and greeted Karume in English. "Why don't you speak Swahili?" Karume asked. The sheepish Soviet turned and left.

The hometown paper back in Wilkes-Barre, Pennsylvania, breathlessly reported in a piece entitled "Carlucci Aids New Nation; He Handles Swahili Language Fluently" that the "linguistic ability of Frank Carlucci, Jr., son of Mr. and Mrs. Frank Carlucci, Bear Creek, may be a factor in the new African nation Tanzania leaning toward the West rather than coming under the influence of the Communist orbit . . . Carlucci's fluent use of Swahili, a native African language, has aided the former local resident the confidence of Tanzania officials in himself and the United States." The article goes on to reference the fact that in a conversation with Zanzibari President Karume and the East German ambassador to Zanzibar, "Carlucci's fluent command of the African language found favor with the heads of the new state, and to the confusion of the Red German official, who had to rely on an interpreter."[28]

The situation in Zanzibar changed significantly when it officially became a part of the neighboring mainland country Tanganyika, another former territory of the British.

The two territories united on April 26, 1964, to create what we now know as Tanzania (TANganyika + ZANzibar + IA). This was a strategic help to the West—the much larger, pro-Western Tanganyika region swallowed the Communist archipelago of Zanzibar, effectively neutralizing the spread of communism in the region. This nullified Soviet and Chinese influence on Zanzibar.

On the matter of the NASA station that my father was instructed to protect: although he spent a lot of time trying to slow down local efforts for its dismantling, the Zanzibari government insisted it needed to be taken down immediately, claiming it was a spy station. My father did his best to stymie this plan, but eventually concluded that it was pointless to try to stop the locals from destroying it. As for his mission to steer clear of controversy, that ended up not going very well either.

A tape emerged of a discussion between my father and Bob Gordon, DCM in Dar es Salaam, that erroneously implied the United States was plotting to overthrow the government in Zanzibar (my father always tied this incident to the East Germans; Gordon blamed the Russians). This led Julius Nyerere, president of Tanzania, to call US Ambassador Bill Leonhart (in tears, apparently—according to my father he cried a lot), demanding that my father leave the country. My father's buddy, President Karume of Zanzibar, could do nothing to help now that his territory was part of Tanzania. Thus, Frank Carlucci was expelled from Zanzibar in January 1965.

In an interview much later, Bob Gordon mulled over the strange course of events.

> [There were] many theories of why [it happened]. One was the fact that I had used the word "ammunition" with Frank and, theoretically, it was interpreted that Frank and I had plotted against the Government of Zanzibar behind the Ambassador's back through direct contacts with CIA . . . Well, baloney . . . I can remember when I was going out as ambassador to Mauritius. I went over to CIA for the usual briefings. Frank Carlucci, at that time, was Deputy Director of CIA. I went up and had a cup of coffee with him. I said, "Frank, now that you've got this job, find out what the hell was the reason."
>
> He said, "I've never been completely satisfied, either. And I can tell you there's not much here because one of the first curiosity files I poked into was that one . . ."
>
> About two years ago, three years ago, I got a letter from Frank telling me that he had met a very high Soviet official at a reception. And this Soviet official told him that they had set us up on this and that they had fiddled with the tape of what we said and didn't say . . . Anyway, this may be the answer, that the Russians set us up.[29]

Another account of the mishap chalked it up to "a comedy of African errors" in which my father was "overheard telephoning his superior about plans to celebrate the new African nation's first anniversary. 'Bring in some big guns,' said the young officer, hopeful that Soapy Williams, assistant secretary of state for African affairs, might attend. The deliberate misinterpretation of that conversation was acknowledged by the prime minister of

Zanzibar, who was using this incident as a chance to parade his power over the great USA."[30]

Whatever the truth, it went down as a piece of memorable Foreign Service lore in my father's career. What happened next was also a potential hiccup in his career:

> The Director General of the Foreign Service, Ambassador Joseph Palmer, called me in. His desk was totally clean except for my personnel file sitting in the middle. Palmer got right to the point. He said, "Young man, you're obviously bright and you'll probably go to the top of the Foreign Service, but you must learn to fit into the system. You're too freewheeling."
>
> I replied, "I don't want to fit into the system."

My father wound up going five years without a promotion. He didn't feel there was a direct blowback from being caught on tape and declared persona non grata in Zanzibar, but the fact that it happened was far from ideal.

My father was next instructed to learn Italian in preparation for a posting as a transportation officer in Rome, but he never ended up going. Transportation officer isn't the most glamorous of assignments, but Rome is considered a plum posting—and if the State Department was concerned about his "freewheeling" nature, perhaps they decided instead to place my father somewhere in the world where he could calm down a bit.

A friend of my father's in the Latin American Bureau, Powhatan Barber, suggested my father speak to US Ambassador to Brazil Lincoln Gordon, a distinguished academic who later became president of Johns Hopkins University. Gordon had previously been a key figure in distributing Marshall Plan aid to rebuild post–World War II Europe. My father recalled:

> It was a strange interview. Gordon asked me where I went to school, and I gave the right answer. I then asked him about conditions in Brazil. Half an hour later he was still talking, and I hadn't said another word. After we broke up, he reportedly called me brilliant. His efforts to have me assigned as principal officer in Brasilia failed, but he was successful in getting me assigned to the embassy in Rio provided I was "buried in the political section." That seemed like the best prospect at the time, so I accepted.

Joe Palmer allowed my father to go to Brazil with the caveat that he must be buried in the bowels of the system. Hence my father's five years without a promotion.

Brazil had recently experienced a dramatic regime change after the 1964 military coup that overthrew President João Goulart. Lincoln Gordon had been instrumental during this period as the primary US interlocutor on the ground. His reporting of the situation in Brazil spurred on US fears that Brazil would become the China or Russia of South America.[31]

Goulart was a left-leaning reformist president who enacted radical reforms aimed at alleviating the plight of lower-class

Brazilians. The military and conservatives in the country, notably in the conservative Catholic community, were opposed to Goulart and his apparently communist leanings.[32] This caught the attention of the US government, which supported the Brazilian Armed Forces' overthrow of Goulart.

Previously, during the Cuban Missile Crisis, President John F. Kennedy had called on Goulart to assist with an invasion of Cuba, if necessary. Goulart refused, making an enemy of Kennedy and instilling distrust between the two men. Kennedy became convinced Goulart was leading Brazil toward becoming a communist state. This certainly played into the US support of the Brazilian military coup in 1964.[33] The coup installed a military dictatorship friendly to the United States, which lasted until 1985.

Thus, when my father arrived in Brazil in July of 1965, he walked into a fresh military dictatorship, albeit one that was friendly toward the United States. At least for once my father arrived after the action, not right before or in the middle of it! But this was also not the "quiet outpost" that perhaps the State Department had sought to place him in.

The living was good in Brazil. My father spoke longingly of the weather, the people, and the tennis whenever he reflected on his time there. (He of course also learned to speak Portuguese—achieving a fluency rating three weeks after arriving.) As my father put it, "The Brazilians have several things of which they are enamored: soccer, the beach, and women. Brazilian women are absolutely gorgeous. Tennis is nearly perfect with clay courts and ball boys. Indeed, most players wouldn't step on the court without them." My half brother, too, has positive, though limited, memories of the experience, given that he was three when they arrived and six when they left.

My father had been in Brazil about two or three months when the embassy's executive officer had to return to Washington because of a family health issue. Ambassador Lincoln Gordon asked my father to step in. The plan to bury him deep in the bureaucracy wasn't working out so well. Executive officer is a fairly junior position in rank, but it essentially made my father the chief administrator of the embassy. This was happening at around the same time that Jack Tuthill replaced Lincoln Gordon as ambassador and started to shake things up a bit. One day, Tuthill called my father in. My father recalled he said, "Frank, read this telegram I'm going to send to the State Department." The telegram said that there were far too many Americans in Brazil telling the Brazilians how to run their country. His opinion was that the United States was creating dependency, not independence.

My father had great respect for Jack Tuthill, and the feeling was mutual. One day Tuthill asked my father who the most useless employee at the embassy was. As my father told it:

> I scratched my head and I said—I gave him a name. And he said, "Get rid of him." So, he called me back in about a month later, and he said, "How are you doing on getting rid of Mr. X?"
>
> I said, "Never had a harder job. The whole bureaucracy is defending him."
>
> He said, "I bet it wouldn't take much more to cut the embassy by 50 percent." And I was a bit stunned.
>
> He said, "Let's think about that." And he came back from a two-martini lunch one day and wrote a cable saying, "I want to cut the embassy by 50 percent." He handed it to me and said, "I want you to edit this and send it off,

> and you are the hatchet man." So, we got permission from the State Department to cut the embassy by 50 percent, and I spent another year going about that process. So, I gained a reputation as someone who would cut staff . . .
>
> I became, in fact, the hatchet man for the largest personnel-cutting operation in the Foreign Service. This caught the eye of Richard Nixon, who visited Brazil while I was there. I was his escort officer and we got along well.

This was not to be my father's last stint as "hatchet man," and it would be far from his last interaction with Nixon. In the meantime, he was growing a little frustrated being posted in Brasilia as opposed to Rio. Brasilia has been the official capital of Brazil since 1960, but it was not, and is not, a vibrant cultural hub. Instead, it's a planned administrative city in the middle of the rainforest—carefully laid out, a poster child for efficient municipal systems. Since it is the official capital of the country, the embassies are located there. My father described his frustration flying hours into the interior of Brazil to reach the capital while knowing the real action was taking place in the chaotic and colorful city of Rio de Janeiro instead.

Imagine if Washington, DC, was located in Kansas and never became a proper, culturally vital city, but instead was an empty political capital to which politicians begrudgingly traveled for a few days at a time to conduct their affairs—that's Brasilia in a nutshell. However, my father got to know many Brazilian bureaucrats and politicians on their regular flights back and forth between Brasilia and the country's other major cities, so this annoying commute did have some value. Eventually my father was a commuter too, with an apartment in Brasilia, which he'd travel to regularly, and a house in Rio where his wife and two young kids stayed.

My father continued doing things his own way, as he had at other postings, making local contacts and getting to know the country's movers and shakers. The political counselor at the embassy, Max Krebs, did not like American officials to have direct contact with the Brazilians. He sourced all of his reporting from the newspapers. My father was friends with a junior officer named Robert "Bob" Bentley who was of the opposite opinion. He came to know the Brazilians quite well, and my father would frequently go with Bentley to meetings. This is how my father began to establish his own network of contacts. One of these was a controversial figure named Carlos Lacerda, who had been governor of the State of Guanabara. My father arranged for him to meet with Ambassador Tuthill. This enraged the military government, which called in the ambassador and told him that if my father continued contact with unfriendly elements, he would be asked to leave.

Tuthill remained ambassador throughout my father's time in Brazil (1966–1969) and the two of them grew quite close. As my father recalled:

> Tuthill was not an academic like Gordon but was flamboyant and a pleasure to work for. He liked attractive women. There was a beautiful local Brazilian employee who sat right by his door. The embassy security officer came to me arguing she couldn't sit by his door as she was a local employee and had not been cleared. I said, "She's going to sit by his door."
>
> He said, "Well, then I want to see the ambassador."
>
> I replied, "Be my guest." He went in and saw the ambassador.
>
> Tuthill came out afterwards and asked, "Who was that

guy who just saw me?" I told him he was the embassy's security officer, and Tuthill paused. "Frank, your job is to make sure he never comes on this floor again."

The local employee stayed where she was.

My father liked working with Tuthill—but the work wasn't always fun or easy. One of the projects they collaborated closely on was the staff-reduction project (referred to as Topsy, an *Uncle Tom's Cabin* reference that I think simply insinuates the embassy grew out of control without any conscious thought). When Tuthill would travel away from the embassy, my father felt quite exposed and unpopular with the rank and file—unsurprising for the guy responsible for enacting the largest personnel-cutting operation in the Foreign Service history. A few years later, in 1972, my father would reflect on the program: "Topsy was neither a personnel nor a budget exercise. It was an effort by a perceptive and forceful ambassador to get a grip on his embassy and to move it in concert toward a goal. This goal was to stop doing things for Brazilians and to concentrate on areas in which we could help Brazilians build the institutional capacity to do things for themselves."[34] Under Trump there was a mass exodus from the State Department, but that wasn't a single, orchestrated operation. Instead, Trump's departures marked the result of months of policy decisions and pressure, so I'm pretty sure my father's achievement remains intact.[35] As a State Department colleague, Herbert "Herb" Okun, recalled: "Frank's Operation Topsy eliminated a lot of military brass, the caddies at the golf course, and the drivers in the carpool. It also abolished Frank's job." Apparently, it also "did not contribute to Carlucci's anonymity. The Foreign Service handed him yet another award and was about to put him out to pasture at MIT."[36] Indeed, the State Department planned to get my father out of the field for a while by sending him to get an advanced business degree from the renowned MIT Sloan School of Management.

Then my father paid a fateful visit to an old friend. Donald Rumsfeld had been a friend since Princeton and had visited in his capacity as a congressman while my father was in Brazil. He asked my father to stop by DC, and when my father did, Rumsfeld sprung on him an offer to be assistant director of the Office of Economic Opportunity (OEO) and head of the Community Action Program, a program about which my father admitted to knowing absolutely nothing. My father described the exchange:

> As a courtesy, I stopped to see Rumsfeld in his new job. He surprised me, saying he wanted me to come into OEO and take over the largest portion of OEO, the Community Action Program.
>
> "Don, I don't know a damn thing about poverty."
>
> "Yes," Don said, "but you know how to run things and the president is most impressed with how you scaled down the staff in Brazil." (We actually ended up with a cut of 33 percent, not 50 percent, but that in itself was an achievement.) "As far as your assignment goes," Don said, "we'll break it," and he picked up the phone and called Elliot Richardson who was deputy secretary of state and told Richardson he wanted me to be assigned to OEO.

My dad never did get to MIT.

Instead, a new and quite different chapter in his life began, one that would set the stage for his rise in the US government.

CHAPTER FOUR

ALPHABET SOUP: FROM OEO *to* OMB *to* HEW *and* BEYOND

MY FATHER RETURNED FROM Brazil in early 1969. Instead of heading to MIT, he was set on a very different course. As he put it, working at the OEO meant being "thrust into a vortex of demonstrations, riots, and various other disruptive activities in the US."

The OEO program had been created by President Lyndon B. Johnson in 1964 to eliminate poverty, a lofty and worthy goal, but it was hated by the Republicans for its perceived mismanagement and profligate spending. The Nixon administration came in disliking OEO intensely. Rumsfeld fought off a congressional attempt to eliminate the OEO completely and saved the agency by promising to move more control to the state level. Rumsfeld gave my father instructions to make sure that the OEO's largest program, the Community Action Program, be brought into better cooperation with governors and mayors. As my father recalled:

> I had had my share of problems with demonstrations and confrontations. I developed techniques like keeping my back to the door and turning the heat up in the room. I remember one time I was visiting a Community Action Agency in Oakland. The CEO, Percy Moore, in introducing me, asked my background.
>
> I said, "Foreign Service."
>
> He said, "What's that?"
>
> I said, "That's someone who conducts diplomacy."
>
> He said, "Jesus Christ. Here I thought the president was going to appoint capable people to these jobs."

My father remembered the CAP as a confrontational program, with pictures of Che Guevara on the wall of some of the employees working in the OEO offices.

My father set about streamlining the program by shutting down regional offices, including ones in Minneapolis and Sacramento (requiring the support of then Governor Reagan to fight off Sacramento's mayor). He even closed an office in his hometown of Wilkes-Barre, Pennsylvania. He closed these offices because they weren't showing themselves to be effective at eliminating poverty, and thus were a drain on resources. The idea was to turn the program into more of a service delivery program that empowered local politicians and people to improve their own communities. My father remembered this as a difficult but educational time.

One day Rumsfeld asked my father to interview a young intern on the Hill working for Congressman William Steiger of Wisconsin.

The young man made quite an impression on my father, who recommended that Rumsfeld hire him. The intern was Dick Cheney.

Dick Cheney became Rumsfeld's special assistant, and my father got to know him quite well as they worked very closely together. Little did these three men know they would all end up taking a turn as secretary of defense one day. Nor did anyone else close to my father have an inkling that he would rise that far, though my grandfather was catching on by now that my father wasn't a businessman in the making but had a promising career in domestic and foreign policy.

When my father was selected to help lead OEO in 1970, my grandfather acknowledged in an interview that "it's a great honor for him. He's had a tough job and his new position will be another tough job and very demanding." In the same article that reported this, though, my grandmother had to then add that my father was "somewhat of a pessimist who was always afraid he wouldn't make his marks in school."[37]

One day Rumsfeld called my father in and said he was leaving OEO and recommended to Nixon that my father replace him. My father's first immediate challenge at OEO would come from the state of California, and its governor, Ronald Reagan. In late 1970, Reagan had vetoed funding for California's popular but long controversial statewide rural services program, California Rural Legal Assistance (CRLA). CRLA largely represented the interests of rural farm workers of California and worked against the interest of their employers (a principal source of funding for Reagan). The gubernatorial veto was subject only to the authority of the director of OEO to override the governor's action—in other words, my father's authority. Before Frank Carlucci could even be confirmed into the job, he would be at odds with the future president.

My father would explain his personal motivation for advocating on behalf of legal services in a White House briefing in 1971: "The short history of this program thus far has dramatically revealed the urgent need for such a program. Without legal services, poor individuals are frequently victimized; their collective needs go unadvocated and unheeded; and the counsel and expertise necessary for economic development is often unavailable."[38]

Nonetheless, Governor Reagan called Nixon and said, "Don't let Carlucci override that veto." Reagan was alleging hundreds of cases of misconduct by CRLA attorneys. The governor had "accused the program's attorneys of improperly or illegally interceding in behalf of black militants, criminals, and the promoter of a private rock festival."[39] About the same time, Alan Cranston, a Democratic senator from California who headed the committee approving my father's appointment, called to say that unless my father overrode the veto, he would not be confirmed. Quite a problem!

My father came up with a plan. He named a three-state Supreme Court judge panel (two Republicans and one Democrat) to investigate the some six hundred charges of wrongdoing that Reagan had levied against CRLA. The judges held hearings up and down the state of California. John Ehrlichman, Nixon's domestic advisor, called and said my father should call off the "circus," but he refused.

After about three months, the judges produced a report that stated they could not verify any of the alleged infractions. My father was instantly sued by the CRLA under the Freedom of Information Act in an attempt to get the report. In the meantime, he called Reagan directly asking for a clandestine meeting, which Reagan granted. The only other person present was Ed Meese, Reagan's chief of staff. My father reflected on that meeting years later: "In that meeting I said, 'Governor, I have this report by three Supreme Court justices that says none of your charges is accurate. It's an embarrassing report. I have not yet released it. I can put rhetoric around it that will make it palatable. I'll take all the heat. I'll take the Congressional hearing, and I'll give you the funds for your own legal services program. In return for which, I want the longest grant in CRLA history.'"[40]

Eventually Reagan came around. My father was issued the grant and testified at a very long and contentious hearing. In the end, he was able to fund the longest grant in CRLA history. The solution worked. The legal services battle had left so many scars that everybody was looking for a way to avoid another squabble with Governor Reagan. In the aftermath, my father helped establish a legal services corporation and ensured the establishment of a law school focused on the legal rights of low-income and minority persons, Antioch Law School, by awarding a grant to start it.

In reflecting on this period of time, my father mentioned,

> The main thing that Community Action did that's terribly important was [that it] created a leadership cadre in the poverty community, particularly the minority community. A lot of people in the program rose up to positions of prominence later on. So that was a significant contribution . . . And the CRLA experience, I think, was by and large a healthy experience, because it calmed things down, and taught the lawyers in the legal services program that they couldn't abuse the process . . . it was important to make sure that poor people had access to the law, and if you lost your Social Security benefits and you were impoverished, you virtually had no place to turn. So, the legal services program was certainly

justifiable in taking those kinds of cases . . . a lot of it was just helping out poor people as opposed to the big class action suits that everybody read about.

Before he could properly catch his breath at OEO, my father's mandate at work was about to change again. Other changes were also afoot. My father was forty years old, and his marriage was falling apart. Chip remembers the tension growing between his parents and my father becoming more and more preoccupied and absorbed with his work, perhaps as a way to escape or avoid the troubles at home. Chip was in first grade when the family returned to Washington. As he moved further into his elementary school years, family dinners around the table dwindled and then ceased. My father came home later than he used to and would retreat to his study, working into the wee hours. On weekends he was equally preoccupied. Chip remembers riding to many Little League baseball games on his bike, by himself. Frank and Jean would divorce a few years later, in 1974.

One day in 1971 when my father was at work at OEO, George Shultz, a former secretary of labor and then the director of the Office of Management and Budget (OMB), called my father and offered him a key job in the organization. Shultz was well regarded in the Nixon administration and was the first director of the new OMB, which to this day remains the largest office in the executive branch and controls the budget of the president, making it very influential (think of how the Budget and Appropriations Committee is unusually powerful in Congress—same dynamic). Shultz would go on to become the secretary of the treasury under Nixon from 1972 to 1974, then after a brief stint in the private sector, he returned to government under the Reagan administration as secretary of state.

Shultz is one of only two people to hold four cabinet appointments, and his tenure as secretary of state defined Reagan's foreign policy. He served in this role for six and a half years and is widely known as one of the most popular and successful secretaries of state. Shultz notably pushed Reagan to develop a relationship with the president of the Soviet Union, Mikhail Gorbachev, setting into motion the end of the Cold War. I like to think that he and my father had quite a bit in common, as "Shultz was renowned for his patient, credible and remarkably effective approach to diplomacy, most often eschewing the limelight to defer to the presidents for whom he worked. Along with his straightforward style, he had a hard-driving commitment to solving tangled policy problems and avoiding extreme partisan politics."[41] However, my father was also very close, perhaps even closer, with one of Shultz's longtime rivals, Cap Weinberger.

While my father was considering a move to OMB, Shultz was named treasury secretary and Cap Weinberger replaced Shultz as director of OMB. Weinberger and my father had already developed a good working relationship and Weinberger asked my father to be his deputy.

When my father made it known he was going to follow Weinberger to OMB, President Nixon wrote a glowing note.

> Your letter of July 26 [1971] submitting your resignation as director of the office of economic opportunity has just reached me, and as you have requested, I accept it . . . My regret that you are leaving your present position is more than compensated by the satisfaction that you will be applying your exceptional abilities to an equally important challenge as associate director of the office of management and budget.

> For the past two years you have brought outstanding professional competence and personal dedication to your demanding responsibilities, working tirelessly on behalf of our programs to help the disadvantaged. Your leadership and wise counsel have contributed significantly and effectively to our efforts in meeting the problems of poverty, and you have every reason to take great pride in your many accomplishments.
>
> As you prepare to assume your new position, I want you to know how deeply I have valued the superb job you have done for the administration. Needless to say, you have my very best wishes for continued success in the years ahead.

Not bad for a guy who was tagging along with the president's entourage in Brazil a few years prior.

The rivalry between Shultz and Weinberger would become legendary. A *New York Times* article from 1985 examined the competition between the two men and offered some fascinating insights into their personalities and approaches:

> Shultz, who is sixty-four, is by nature and training a professor, mediator, and private man. He prefers conciliation to confrontation. Often impassive—a colleague describes him as "sphinxlike"—Shultz is a man of enormous self-

> assurance. Weinberger, who is sixty-seven, is a litigator, a politician, altogether more of a public personality. He seems to thrive on confrontation and, like his idol Winston Churchill, can be totally unyielding in defense of principles he considers important, such as sustained growth in the defense budget. Unlike Shultz, Weinberger does not radiate a sense of being at peace with himself and his position.[42]

When my father became the deputy director, the No. 2 guy at OMB, he also became the key go-between of Shultz and Weinberger. The two would often squabble, and Frank found himself in the middle trying to get them to find common ground. This power trio, which would later play a huge role in the Reagan administration, was first assembled in OMB under Nixon.

At OMB my father worked with various agencies to design their budgets. My father recalled that when he presented a budget to Nixon, the president became fixated on shutting down the OEO, the office where my father had just worked. This caused an uproar, but Nixon eventually won out. It took time to wind down OEO such that its functions could be absorbed into other departments.[43]

My father remembered two assignments while serving as deputy director of OMB that were especially noteworthy.

First, Hurricane Agnes hit Northeastern Pennsylvania just before election eve in 1972. It did widespread damage and was the costliest hurricane to hit the United States to date, resulting in 118 fatalities and $3.5 billion in property damage. Twelve states were affected, with the worst damage occurring in New York and Pennsylvania.[44] Almost half of the average annual rainfall total for the Susquehanna River Basin fell in the period of three days. Towns were under several feet of water; hundreds of thousands of people lost their homes or electricity; and hundreds of roads, bridges, and railroads were damaged or destroyed. The flood still currently holds the water level records in numerous places across the state of Pennsylvania. The name Agnes was subsequently retired, the telltale sign of a truly terrible hurricane.[45]

At the time there was no designated government office for handling disaster relief. The role ultimately fell to OMB, specifically, to Frank Carlucci. President Nixon sent a note via his assistant for domestic affairs, John Ehrlichman, telling my father to pull together a relief program. Rather than appointing a "relief czar," my father ended up taking on responsibility for the program himself, traveling to the area to help with rehousing individuals in temporary shelters and providing grants to schools.

As a result of these efforts, Frank received honorary doctorates from several colleges in the area. All the while he was still the deputy director of OMB; overseeing the relief program was additional work on top of his daily responsibilities—an indication of his true commitment to public service.

Amid the seriousness of the disaster relief came a moment of levity. A humorous incident occurred when President Nixon made a last-minute visit to Wilkes-Barre. As my father recalled, on the way out of town, Nixon pointed to a crowd in front of the church.

> "What's that?" he said. I had no idea, it looked like a wedding. When we got abreast of the church, he said, "Stop the car."
>
> The secret service man said, "Where?"
>
> "Right here," said Nixon, "in the middle of the street." Nixon jumped out, bounded up the stairs of the church just as the newly married couple was coming out of the

door. If you ever wanted to see a startled couple, this was it. The groom had the presence of mind to say that when he gets married, he does it right!

Nixon greeted everyone all around and we got back in the car and headed to the airport. He had a flair for this kind of gesture.

Such moments were brief respites from the hard work of disaster relief. The task at hand was truly enormous. What's more, the storm had struck very close to home for my father, quite literally. It destroyed places that were important to him as a young man and affected people he knew personally, though his parents had relocated to Florida a few years earlier. He recounted the following in a memorandum for the president in September of 1972:

> Before you sent me on August 12 to the flooded areas of Pennsylvania as your personal representative, you spelled out definitive instructions in four areas . . . Now, about four weeks later, I report to you as your personal representative about our accomplishments and remaining goals, concentrating on Wyoming Valley, by far the hardest hit area. But also, Mr. President, I report to you as a native of the Valley who has seen childhood friends in despair, neighborhood landmarks crushed and former homes in Forty Fort and Kingston in a pile of rubble. I've walked across the square in Wilkes-Barre back to my office from a meeting three blocks away. It took forty-five minutes. Friends of my family would stop me. Others would shake my hand and say, "Tell the president he's doing great." Some would say thanks. Then there were many who would ask for help.

And help was offered, in the form of several billions in federal aid, of which my father helped to oversee distribution. He also wanted to make sure that the next time such a disaster occurred, people would be better prepared.

In an interview with historian Robert Wolensky my father said, "Of course, what Hurricane Agnes led to was the creation of FEMA . . . I had a role to play and some people have called me the father of FEMA, in that I recommended that there be some kind of agency."[46]

Of all the things my father accomplished as "a daredevil diplomat, an expert budget-whacker and, to presidents and Cabinet secretaries, the indispensable No. 2 man who ran things: the day-to-day affairs of America's anti-poverty programs, its health, education and welfare systems, its intelligence services and its military operations,"[47] and in his long and successful private sector career, he still recalled those months coming to the aid of his native Pennsylvanians in the wake of disaster as one of the most important tasks of his career. I would ask him later in life what he was most proud of, and he always mentioned the Hurricane Agnes relief efforts.

Another challenge would come along soon thereafter. The second-most memorable and difficult project my father recalled from his time at OMB had to do with the government's interactions with the American Indian Movement, which was gaining momentum at the time. In the week leading up to the 1972 presidential election, a number of caravans of Native Americans began to move across the country in protest of mistreatment. Poor housing, underfunded schools, and health crises on reservations led to a protest against the federal government for failure to honor treaties with their tribal governments. Dubbed "The Trail of Broken Treaties," in reference to the Trail of Tears, five hundred to eight hundred Native Americans traveled to Washington, DC, making stops along the way and spreading their stories.

However, no housing arrangements had been made, forcing the protesters to sleep in local church basements. When they arrived in Washington, the protesters went to the Bureau of Indian Affairs (BIA) and asked to use their auditorium and kitchen. The BIA refused. The Native Americans claimed this was *their* bureau and refused to leave—for six days. Protesters erected teepees in front of the building and hung a sign reading "Native American Embassy," leading to multiple confrontations with government officials. This protest was seen as one of "the most important acts of Indian resistance since Little Big Horn," according to prominent scholars who study Native American resistance.[48] About $700,000 in damages were reported, and key records housed in the BIA were destroyed or lost.

Nixon was clear he did not want this protest to turn violent. Leonard Garment, acting special counsel to Nixon, negotiated with the Native Americans alongside my father. They realized there was a major obstacle preventing the Native Americans from leaving: they had no means to return home. My father came up with the idea of paying for their way home, so he walked into the building with $65,000 in cash and handed it out to the protesters.

A statement my father wrote to Congress gives insight into his thoughts and decision-making process during this high-stakes and volatile situation:

> I was advised that there were both hardline and moderate elements among the Indians, with the former fully prepared to turn the BIA building into a funeral pyre at midnight, November 6, three hours after our first scheduled

> meeting . . . such a prediction seemed to me to be overdrawn at first, but it became increasingly likely as I learned more of the facts . . . our choices at the eleventh hour were severely constrained; we had to chart a course between intransigence vs. almost certain violence, between substantive concessions vs. encouragement to militants. Negotiation could lead to either violence or unwarranted concession.

He went on to enumerate the goals of the negotiation and the possible results that he and other government officials wanted to avoid. He then concluded the following:

> By any reasonable account of discussions we avoided almost every concession or result we intended to avoid. There are those who have chided us for not taking "firm and immediate action"—for not removing the Indians "by force if necessary." The TBT people were overwrought. Some were emotional to the apparent point of irrationality. Leaders talked of martyrdom, while outsiders talked of tough action and removal by force . . . We all too frequently have seen how "firm and immediate action" can lead to tragedy, even with the best intentions by law enforcement officers—Kent State, Southern University. Such events—once set in motion—have a force and logic of their own. They are sometimes impossible to control.
>
> Those who were in the building during the discussions or immediately after the Indians' departure recall only too well the potential for violence to get out of hand—threats by the Indians to dynamite and burn the building, reports of dynamite being seen, and smell of gasoline spread over

> papers in the halls, pictures of Indians with clubs and other weapons, Molotov cocktails in offices on the third floor ready for use, typewriters stacked on parapets on the roof and at the head of the stairs on the top floor, obviously there to hurl down.
>
> When I visited the building at 7:15 p.m. on November 8 as the Indians were leaving, I saw a baby who couldn't have been more than six months old. There were many such children in the building at the height of the confrontation, so many in fact that the Indians had established a nursery on the third floor. How senseless the sacrifice of these children and their misguided parents would have been in the presumed interest of teaching a few militant extremists a lesson. One more chapter in the unfortunate history of [the] relationship with the Indians would have been written, never to be erased.
>
> In a day and a half of lengthy, deliberate discussions, we brought the matter to a close without loss of life or serious injuries. We had substituted conversation for confrontation, something that perhaps ought to have been done a century earlier.

This is the type of event that could have made for an entry in the history books, for horrible reasons. Instead, as so often happens when the worst does not occur, it's been swept aside and largely forgotten.

My father moved on, too. His stint at OMB came to an end in the same way as many of his roles did: when superiors who liked and trusted him got moved up or around, and they wanted a trusted colleague to come with them.

Nixon won a landslide re-election in 1972. One of his first acts was to fire his entire cabinet. According to my father, firing everyone "was a fairly typical Nixon move. He liked to startle people. He liked to shake things up. He liked to be dramatic. He liked to be tough. It fulfilled all those requirements."[49]

The president called Cap Weinberger and asked him to become the secretary of the Department of Health, Education, and Welfare (HEW), which has since been renamed the Department of Health and Human Services (HHS). Weinberger asked my father to be the under secretary. Effectively, my father was the one running HEW despite being the No. 2 man at the agency, as Weinberger was often off serving in his role as a special counselor to the president. Weinberger knew this would be the case when he asked my father to fill the role.

I now see my father's relationship with Weinberger as foreshadowing one he would later have with Colin Powell, one of his closest friends and most treasured colleagues. When my father and Powell first got to know each other, my father had just left the CIA to become deputy secretary of defense. He asked Powell to be his military assistant. He could see that Powell was bright and capable and likely to go far in his career. And so, he trusted him, as an equal—the same way Weinberger had put his trust in my father some years before. It was in part from Weinberger that my father learned (and saw firsthand) that a strong executive team was vitally important. A single individual cannot stand alone in decision making but must learn to rely on the good decisions of the people he chooses to work with.

Certainly, in a huge bureaucracy, you have to know who you can trust and who you can rely on. That certainly was the case when my father went to work at the HEW. It was a behemoth organization with one hundred programs that administered various forms of social welfare programs, ranging from education to health care.

My father recounted a story of clashing with then Governor of Georgia Jimmy Carter, who vetoed a program my father supported. Initially, Weinberger didn't want to overrule Carter's veto, but my father convinced him to, with the prediction that Carter was likely to disappear from the political scene in short order:

> Head Start, one of HEW's flagship programs, had made a grant to Georgia which then Governor Jimmy Carter had vetoed. The secretary of HEW could override the veto. The HEW staff appealed to me. I went to Cap, who had been brought up through state government and was a firm believer that the federal government should not interfere with the states. But I told him it was a good program and we had to save it. He said, "Let's call Jimmy Carter." So, we called Governor Carter, who was very pleasant, but said no he wouldn't withdraw his veto. When we hung up, I turned to Cap and said, "Cap, he's a lame duck governor, you'll never hear from him again, override the veto." And with that Cap overrode the veto!

Pretty funny, in hindsight.

Although he was crossing paths with many people who were making history at this time, I like to think that the most important person my dad got to know while at HEW was my mother, Marcia McMillan Myers. They had first met briefly when my father was at OEO and she was working in the White House Liaison Office. She already had a reputation as a hard worker and a straight shooter. When my father started at HEW, he asked her to come over and act as the White House liaison there, and as special assistant. During this time they formed a friendship and then a deeper bond.

My mother was not a born-and-bred part of the Beltway set. She came to DC on her own, from Madison, Wisconsin, to intern on the Hill while she was still in college. As soon as she graduated, she moved to Washington permanently, motivated by a passion for politics and a drive to see something bigger than her family's midwestern world. She was hard to miss in a crowd of suits: Her fiery red hair was matched only by her social and political acumen, and in personality she was my father's opposite in almost every way. Besides being fifteen years his junior, she was outgoing and he was quiet; she was impulsive and he was deliberate. However, they were both ambitious and dedicated. And more than anything, my mother deeply respected and admired my father.

Around the same time, my father's respect for the then president was on the wane. My father became increasingly disenchanted with the Nixon administration as the Watergate investigations heated up. He and Weinberger discussed whether or not to resign, but ultimately, they agreed to stick it out a little longer. My father was in Aspen when he heard that Nixon had resigned. Gerald "Jerry" Ford, Nixon's vice president, became the president. My father knew Jerry well. In his memoirs he recounts a story of when Ford came to visit HEW and somehow my father was locked in a bathroom.

> President Ford . . . quickly went around to all the cabinet departments. He came over to HEW. Cap was away so I introduced him [to others]. Funny story, because the president was en route, and I went into the bathroom in the office next to mine. I don't know why I used that one, but I couldn't get out. There I was, the acting secretary of HEW

> with the president on his way to HEW and I was pounding on the door of the bathroom trying to get out. Finally, I got out. It was a moment of panic. I got down there just in time to greet the president. He came over and talked to the employees and was very reassuring.
>
> Jerry Ford was able to pick up immediately because he knew the federal budget very well. He is [a] greatly underrated president. He understood all the HEW programs. When you wanted to appeal your budget mark, you would sit down directly with Jerry Ford and he, without notes or assistants, would talk about what the program ought to be. He moved in without missing a beat as far as we were concerned.[50]

Another anecdote my father recalled describes the type of leader he found Ford to be.

> When I was undersecretary of HEW, Cap was on travel, and a bill had reached the president's desk. It was a social services bill, and I was summoned over to brief the president—just basically Jerry Ford and me. I don't think anybody else was in the room. And he said, "Frank, what about this bill?"
>
> And I said, "Mr. President it's a bad bill. Let me tell you why it's a bad bill." And I went through it piece by piece and I said, "But I must tell you, if you veto it, you'll be overridden in a minute."
>
> He said, "Well, that doesn't concern me. If it's a bad bill, I must veto it." And he vetoed it, and he was overridden in a minute. An extraordinary man."[51]

Yes, my father was an unabashed fan of President Ford. In an interview from 2009 he said, "Our country was in deep trouble [after the Watergate scandal] and to have a man of his integrity and courage step up to a non-elected presidency and make the decisions he made is a blessing for all of us. I think he should be remembered with great respect and reverence."[52]

As much as he admired and respected Ford and enjoyed working with him, soon my father would find himself far from the White House once again.

CHAPTER FIVE

BRINGING PORTUGAL BACK *from the* BRINK

WHILE MY FATHER WAS working at HEW, the Cold War was heating up. One flashpoint in the crisis was tiny Portugal, a member of NATO. Secretary of State Henry Kissinger thought Portugal was lost to the Communists. It was true that the prime minister there and many of his ministers were communists. The president of Portugal was also a communist sympathizer. Kissinger wanted to take a tough line and ostracize Portugal, and the US ambassador to Portugal at the time did not favor that, so Kissinger removed him. Soon enough my father got a call from the State Department, asking him to take on the role.

It was a tough assignment, especially since the media was portraying Portugal as totally lost, a feeling shared by many in the diplomatic corps. But my father always liked a challenge and he agreed to take the job. He took a refresher course in Portuguese and flew to Lisbon about a week after confirmation. When he landed, he held his first press conference at the airport in Portuguese. That created quite an impression, since no American ambassador prior to him had spoken the language, nor had they made themselves available to the Portuguese press, which was quite leftist.

My father's posting as ambassador to Portugal undoubtedly changed his life—and I have it to thank for mine, as it was during this time that he married my mom. It raised some eyebrows for him to bring her along on his posting. Her official role and title was special assistant to the ambassador. Everyone knew that my mother was capable and talented, so it wasn't that she couldn't handle the role. But everyone could also see that her being in Portugal had far more to do with my parents' plans to spend their lives together than with my mother's interest in foreign policy.

John Garon, a Foreign Service Officer who served in Portugal with my father and became a dear friend, remembers their arrival on the embassy scene quite vividly. In a letter to me he recalled:

> I learned that I would have to give up [oversight of] the personnel officer position, occupied at the time by a first-tour officer (and future ambassador), Jane Becker. The State Dept. [then] created the position of "special assistant to the ambassador" to be occupied by political appointee Marcia Myers . . . I also learned, by phone, that Ms. Myers was to be lodged "in an apartment/house, with a garage and new furnishings, located near the ambassador's residence."
>
> Years later, when I told your dad what we had to do to prepare for your mom's arrival, he was appalled. He had never instructed or asked anyone to issue any instructions

> to the embassy. In fact, he had specifically [requested] that Marcia was to be treated as any other employee, and to make sure we knew of his wishes.
>
> Across the board, female employees and the wives of the American staff were far more appalled by Marcia's assignment than the husbands or male employees. Some vitriol I heard was motivated by the sacking of Jane Becker, universally liked and recognized as an outstanding FSO by everyone. When your father was assigned to Lisbon, the Dept. of State was beginning to recognize the plight of women in the Foreign Service. Some of us knew women FSOs who had been forced to resign their commission when they married another FSO, male, of course.[53]

My mother approached the situation delicately and respectfully. She made it clear that she was there to work together with others, not to push them out of the way. Her welcoming attitude and social ease meant my mom soon found her footing at the embassy and at the residence, which was later renamed Casa Carlucci.

When my parents got married on April 15, 1976, it was not a huge gathering with lots of pomp and circumstance. Instead, it took place on a rocky outcrop in the Mediterranean. Portugal was still a staunchly Catholic country at the time, and the fact that my father had been married previously made it uncomfortable, if not impossible, for them to have a proper wedding. They discovered they could marry on Gibraltar, given its status as a British territory, so off they went. The only person in attendance other than two court-appointed witnesses was now twelve-year-old Chip. Chip had come over to spend a summer with my father and ended up spending the entirety of my father's tour as ambassador living with him in Lisbon. Before leaving for Gibraltar, Chip asked a cook at the residence for some uncooked rice, which he secretly smuggled on the trip to throw at my parents as they emerged from exchanging their vows in front of a justice of the peace. On my parents' wedding night, the three of them went out to dinner and had a steak—a very good one, in Chip's recollection.

This was an eventful time for my family, not only personally, but professionally as well. It's not an exaggeration to say that my father's time as the American ambassador to Portugal changed the course of Cold War history as Portugal teetered between communism and democracy. My father's deft handling of the fragile situation exemplified what Senator Frank Church urged at the time: "We need a foreign policy that is willing to accept the grays, to be tolerant of the emerging, and to be patient with those somewhere in the middle."[54] Or, as the future French President Mitterrand put it even more clearly, the United States had some mistakes to answer for, and some bad feelings to put right around the world. Portugal was one place it could do so. As Mitterrand said:

> Portugal may signal a change in America's attitude, a new tolerance for different approaches to democracy. Unhappily, the American image has been tarnished by your foreign policy, not only in Vietnam but all over the world. The old image of the US as the champion of free thought and free action has been supplanted by one that sees the US creaking along with old-fashioned ideas and outdated policies. Unhappily we see you as constantly bolstering the right, sometimes fascists, often militarists. The Portuguese are wary of becoming another Chile [which had recently fallen under the rule of a ruthless dictator, Pinochet]. But

> in fact, the United States has come, not rapidly, but come nevertheless, to an understanding of Portugal. And that fact has been appreciated.[55]

That fact that the United States came to an understanding of Portugal had much to do with my father's deft handling of a situation where "Secretary of State Henry Kissinger told Portuguese leader Mário Soares he thought Portugal was doomed to Communist rule."[56] Not so fast.

Understanding the significance of the moment my father arrived on the scene in Portugal requires a quick trip through the country's history.[57] Portugal has officially been a republic since 1910, when a parliamentary democracy was established. In 1926, a bloodless military coup overthrew this Portuguese First Republic, replacing it with the Portuguese Second Republic: the *Ditadura Militar* (military dictatorship) from 1926 to 1933, and the *Estado Novo* from 1933 to 1974. Although a "republic" in name, this was an authoritarian government, which was led by António de Oliveira Salazar from 1932 to 1968 (thirty-six years!). During his dictatorship, democratic-like institutions existed merely as a facade and were in fact stacked with supporters of Salazar; political freedoms were suppressed, sometimes ruthlessly by military police, and public attention was concentrated on economic recovery.

Although flawed, the pervasive idea among top US diplomats at the time was that it was better for countries like Fascist Spain and dictator-run Portugal and Greece to remain a part of the US orbit; too much pressure from us to push them toward true democracy was avoided for fear of it backfiring. If we alienated such governments, the perceived danger was that they would quickly run to the side of the Russians. The United States at the time was also engaged in multiple international crises, including ongoing Cold War skirmishes, the US withdrawal from Vietnam, the domestic backlash to Watergate, and the Israel-Arab clash of October 1973. Tiny Portugal was hardly a top priority. Given its NATO membership, it was also seen as a largely reliable ally—until domestic unrest forced a regime change.

Starting in the 1960s, a series of independence movements broke out in the Portuguese colonies of Mozambique, Congo, Angola, and Guinea. The Salazar and Caetano regimes had to divert more and more of Portugal's budget to maintain these colonies and to fund the military at a time when many other European countries had freed their colonies. This led Portugal to become politically ostracized; it faced arms embargoes and other international sanctions.

By the early 1970s, thousands of left-wing students and anti-war activists had fled the country, making right-wing militants the dominant force in the Portuguese school system and solidifying the power of the authoritarian regime. Opposition eventually arose on the left with the formation of the Armed Forces Movement (MFA), a group of lower-ranking, politically free-thinking officers who resented changes to military laws. This opposition would eventually coalesce to become the driving force behind a revolution.

On April 23, 1974, American diplomat Bob Bentley met with a close advisor of Portuguese Prime Minister Marcello Caetano. Bentley learned that the PM planned to resign in the next forty-eight hours, due to a growing military movement, and that the Portuguese president intended to form a new government. The next day Bentley wrote a letter to Secretary of State Henry Kissinger that read: "There will be regime change in Portugal." On April

25 Bentley was called into the State Department to meet with the intelligence and research desk officer, as the Nixon administration had in fact just learned of a revolution occurring in Portugal.

The United States was said to have been largely unaware of the impending revolution, but this is a bit disingenuous. It was clear that discontent was fomenting, and the situation escalated after the publication of *Portugal e o Futuro*, a book by conservative military general Antonio de Spínola that resulted in Caetano removing de Spínola from the command of Portuguese forces in Guinea. The public began to take sides, and over the coming days, the ouster and disappearance of de Spínola and another officer, Costa Gomes, further increased the tension in the atmosphere. A small military rebellion of two hundred to three hundred soldiers arose on March 15 from northern military barracks but fell apart after being pushed back by loyalists. A telegram sent by the US ambassador who preceded my father, Stuart Nash Scott, stated that this military coup attempt had "revealed major divisions within [the] Portuguese military." He concluded that, due to Caetano's weakened position, there would be further problems. Kissinger instructed Scott and the US embassy in Portugal to keep their distance from de Spínola. Scott pushed back, saying that de Spínola's views were so pervasive that it would have been impossible to be a part of the conversation about Portugal's future without taking a position on him.

The Revolution of the Carnations began on April 25, 1974, after a thousand junior officers known as the Captains signed a petition against the current government.

This insider's perspective from the US embassy at this time comes again from John Garon (who refers to my father as FCC, a moniker that would stick with him the rest of his life):

I'm probably the only Foreign Service Officer (FSO) still alive today who served at the embassy pre-FCC and who stayed for a few years after his arrival, so it might be useful to paint a tapestry of how Embassy Lisbon operated prior to April 25, 1974.

For five decades prior to the "carnation revolution," Portugal had been governed by only two right wing dictators: Salazar and Caetano. Political dissent was strictly forbidden, so internal Portuguese political life did not exist. Consequently, Embassy Lisbon was a sleepy outpost where little ever happened. For FSOs, it was a good place to plan one's retirement; it was also an ambassadorial sinecure for political donors, or as a reward for outstanding FSOs who spoke Portuguese . . . In 1973, the State Department was still an "Old Boys Club," where whom you knew was more important than what you knew.

FCC's predecessor, Stuart N. Scott, a retired New York lawyer, had been chosen for the Lisbon posting by his former law partner, then Secretary of State William Rogers. On April 25, 1974, with the exception of DCM Richard St. Francis Post and Labor Attaché Mel Povenmire, Scott and the entire senior staff, and spouses, were on the last day of a three-day official visit of every island in the Azores, a first for an American ambassador.

The entire group was housed at Lajes Air Base. Early morning April 25, ready to fly back to Lisbon, we were informed there had been a coup d'état and all Portuguese airports were closed. Ambassador Scott decided to take a military flight to Washington and brief the White House and Secretary Kissinger on what he knew about the situation, which was less than what the *New York Times* knew.

The 1974 Portuguese coup was a colossal American intelligence failure and a fatal blow to Scott's tenure as ambassador. For fifty years, not wanting to offend the ruling Salazar/Caetano régimes, embassy officials suffered from "localitis," an illness that afflicts diplomats who cozy up exclusively to the ruling generals and admirals, ignoring the majors, captains, and lieutenants, not to mention the average soldier, the people actually fighting, and dying, in Angola and Mozambique in Portugal's case.

DCM Dick Post was a so-so administrator, but very capable at reading the Portuguese political tea leaves. By phone, he advised Scott, still at Lajes, that in spite of the bellicose noises emanating from the left and coup leaders, Portugal was still a conservative country that wanted a change, but not the one offered by the Communists. Scott agreed with Post's analysis and so told the president and Kissinger.

In late 1973, Secretary Rogers had been Macchiavellied out of his job by Henry Kissinger, who did not believe the reassurances of Scott or Dick Post. Kissinger was convinced that Portugal had gone "communist" and should be expelled from NATO. He sacked DCM Post shortly after the coup, and Scott's untimely visit to the Azores provided Kissinger with the cover he needed to fire Scott. [58]

Despite repeated radio appeals from the "Captains of April" (another term for the MFA) advising civilians to stay home, thousands of Portuguese took to the streets in popular support of the uprising. A central gathering point was the Lisbon flower market, then richly stocked with carnations, which were in season. Some of the insurgents put carnations in their gun barrels, an image that was broadcast on television worldwide, and that gave the revolution its name. Only four civilians were killed as the Caetano government absconded from power.

Initially the news of the revolution was received favorably in Washington. Kissinger had come around to the idea that de Spínola was a decorated war hero with pragmatic approaches to decolonization and military reform. Perhaps the United States could work with him after all.

A turbulent period in Portuguese politics ensued, as multiple governing bodies and political figures attempted to wrest control of the country. The First Provisional Government came into power, with two notable Communists as prominent figures (Álvaro Cunhal and Avelino Gonçalves).

Henry Kissinger saw the spread of communism in Europe as a contagion that threatened not only our alliances (even going so far as to say NATO would fall apart), but also the future of the United States. In his memoirs, Kissinger paints a grim picture of an isolated United States surrounded by countries that did not share its values, should communism continue to spread unchecked. In Italy, the Italian Christian Democrats were contemplating an alliance with the Italian Communist Party—Kissinger felt that if either Portugal or Italy fell to communism, the other would fall next, starting a cascade of communism that would spread across Europe. Ambassador Scott disagreed, and his perceived "softness" on the subject, from Kissinger's viewpoint, likely cost Scott his job. The irony is that the incoming ambassador, my father, agreed with Scott that Portugal could be "saved."

My father's nomination for the ambassadorship was recommended by Secretary of State Kissinger, in conversation with President Ford on October 18, 1974, and was recorded as follows:

> Kissinger: Our Portuguese Embassy is a disaster. [Stuart Nash] Scott just got there. He was legal advisor just before I came to State, and I wanted someone else. It would be unjust to remove him, but we really have no choice. Frank Carlucci would be great.
>
> President Ford: I was thinking of him for OMB. But if we need him there, let's do it. We can get someone else for OMB.
>
> Kissinger: Okay, I will talk to him then.
>
> President Ford: Let's go ahead.[59]

My father was appointed the US ambassador to Portugal on December 9, 1974. He presented his credentials on January 24, 1975. News of his impending arrival was not exactly welcomed by embassy staff, given his reputation as a maverick and the fact that he was arriving in the middle of an unsettled political situation. In his letter to me, John Garon recalls:

> FCC's nomination was greeted with some fear and apprehension by the embassy's senior staff . . .
>
> Kissinger had been quoted by *TIME*, that he was sending "tough guy" Frank Carlucci to Lisbon, with instructions to . . . not coddle the commies now in charge of Portugal's destiny. Already, the CIA chief of station, the defense, Army and Air Force attaches, the economic

and political counselors had received word that they were being replaced . . . SOON. I called Human Resources in Washington: "Am I next?"

"Probably! Carlucci wants to bring his own section chiefs," was the answer. At this point, morale at the embassy was at a nadir.

A state of uncertainty, not just about careers but families, affected everyone. Those already told to leave had children in school, Christmas was coming, etc., so the rumor mill went into overdrive. When it rains, it pours: the State Department's own Darth Vader, Wells Stabler, State's country director for IB (Iberia), soon visited Lisbon, ostensibly to fill us in on the details behind the nomination . . .

A friend in the Department had warned me not to trust Stabler. I spent over one hour listening to him tell me about FCC, whom he did not like. Stabler, it turned out, had lobbied for the Lisbon ambassador's job. Then he told me about the loss of my HR officer to make room for Marcia Myers, FCC's "special assistant." He added that FCC had not yet decided my fate, adding that it might depend on how my section treated Marcia! . . . FCC was just an amalgam of rumors and stories of his past exploits, and no one in the loop, not even Stabler, had ever met Marcia Myers.

Stabler turned out to be 100 percent wrong in his assessment of Frank C. Carlucci and Marcia Myers.[60]

The night of my father's arrival, the first of many demonstrations took place. The embassy was surrounded. My father got in an old, beat-up station wagon, which he had requested for his transportation to his post (instead of the ambassador's limousine).

He asked his DCM, Herb Okun, who had served with him in Brazil, to join him, and they drove through the crowd waving cheerily. Some of the Portuguese waved back . . .

About two months later, in March, there was a failed coup attempt. The head of Portuguese security, Otelo Saraiva de Carvalho, went on television to say that the American ambassador should leave. My father called him to be certain of what he said. He confirmed it.

My father described this incident in detail in an interview:

> There was a coup attempt, I guess it was a right-wing coup attempt, nobody knows much about it, on the 15th of March, 1975. That evening we were all in the embassy and there were demonstrators out in the street. Otelo Saraiva de Carvalho went on television and said that the American ambassador had been behind the coup attempt and that he had no intention of protecting me. I got him on the telephone and said, "First of all I want to make sure that is what you said," and he said, "Yes."
>
> I said, "Well, you understand that that is the equivalent of declaring the American ambassador persona non grata."
>
> He said, "No, I didn't understand that."
>
> I said, "Well, that is not your job."
>
> He said, "What is my job?"
>
> I said, "Your job is to protect the American ambassador and you made me a virtual target."
>
> We went on in that vein for a while and he finally said, "What should I do?"
>
> I said, "Well, you had better protect me." To my surprise he sent some troops over to my house. I was always

> nervous as to whether they were there to protect me or for some other purpose.
>
> Sure, there were a number of threats and there were demonstrations virtually two or three times a week. At one point they were on the verge of breaking into the embassy and I issued orders to use tear gas. At one point they caught me in my automobile and started rocking it. The State Department sent me a lot of security . . . In fact, I became fairly close to some of the original coup plotters, Melo Antunes and Vitor Alves, even Vasco Lorenzo. I spent a lot of time with them and was convinced that even they were not happy with the turn the events had taken, even though they were all on the left side of the spectrum. I think those contacts at least helped to neutralize them, if nothing else.[61]

Sometimes tensions ran high. Chip remembers that fact being hard to ignore when a Marine was suddenly escorting him to school. But whatever turmoil my father was dealing with in global geopolitics never stopped him from going about his regular life: jogging, playing tennis on the court at the residence (lore has it he was permitted to install it only under the auspices of it serving as a helicopter landing pad for security reasons), making weekend trips to the beach with his wife and son whenever possible. It wasn't just about having downtime: when going about these everyday activities, my father was also meeting people who gave him greater perspective on what the average Portuguese citizen saw, thought about, and wanted for their country. My father played tennis with a former national champion and also with his security detail.

The living had long been good for Americans at the embassy in Lisbon, but the work—not so much. Larry Eagleburger, the under secretary for administration at the time, told my father that Lisbon was the worst embassy in the world when my father first arrived. It was seen as a sleepy, undermanned post, and the person doing the main political reporting was reputed to be subpar.

My father's first priority was to shape up the embassy, which he delegated in part to Herb Okun. My father made himself available to the press at the time—he was told he put himself out there perhaps a bit too much, according to Washington. He set out to get to know the political figures, often meeting two or three a day, and also got to know leaders in the church since he recognized the important role Catholicism played in Portuguese society.[62]

He soon made his own assessment of the situation in Portugal, after visiting with a large number of Portuguese leaders, and it differed significantly from Kissinger's. My father concluded that Portugal would not stay Communist for the following reasons: geographic and economic ties to Europe; NATO ties; the hard-working, conservative nature of the Portuguese people; and most of all, the influence of the Catholic church. The village priests in the north had great sway, and when they began telling the farmers that the Communists would take their land and their cattle, a counterrevolution formed.

When my father reported his views to Washington, he heard that Kissinger was not happy. Rather than hiding out, my father flew to Washington to discuss the situation. My father told Kissinger that the hardline approach would not work, and that he felt they should push for free democratic elections. He also suggested that he should avoid statements that my father felt were pushing Portugal into the arms of the Communists.

According to my father, Kissinger said, "If you're so goddamn smart, you make the statements."

To which my dad replied, "Thank you. I will."

Kissinger's staff told my father that Kissinger would not budge, so my father knew he had to try to go around him. My father went to Donald Rumsfeld and told him what was going on.

Apparently, Rumsfeld just said, "You two need to work it out."

My father was adept at reading relationships, knowing when to push and when to defer. It was no different with the secretary of state than with anyone else. In the end, my father convinced Kissinger to believe in Portugal's moderate democratic forces, and to trust that they could come out as the winners in the aftermath of the Portuguese revolution. Kissinger was not alone in his strong belief that Portugal was destined to become a communist nation, another Soviet puppet and satellite country. There was a special danger in the idea of a NATO ally falling to communism.

The summer of 1975, known in Portugal as the Hot Summer of 1975 (*Verão Quente de 1975*), was an angsty season charged with the undercurrent of the threat of civil war and chaos. Amid obvious government dysfunction Portugal was clearly moving leftward in its politics. The Portuguese Communist Party was populating positions of power at the local and national levels and gaining influence with the labor unions.

As ambassador, my father was instrumental in tamping down passions on both sides during this tumultuous time: keeping the United States from engaging with Portugal in too confrontational a manner and helping gently steer the Portuguese people away from anarchy and toward democracy. A key relationship that helped him achieve these aims was with Mário Soares, a Socialist foreign minister who would go on to serve as prime minister of Portugal from 1976 to 1978, and from 1983 to 1985, and as the seventeenth president of Portugal from 1986 to 1996. My father clearly recalled their first meeting:

> I will never forget it. It was an evening and I had been there only a day or two. I think he was foreign minister at the time. He was very down. When he left, Herb Okun and I turned to each other and said, "What have we gotten ourselves into?"
>
> The Portuguese are wonderful people but a little pessimistic by nature, fatalistic. It is always hard to cheer them up and get them to look at the positive side of things. I set about deliberately to do that, to convince them that things were not lost. I had had a little experience doing that when I headed for Richard Nixon the disaster relief effort after Hurricane Agnes . . . And it was much the same kind of thing in Portugal. Expressing faith in the Portuguese people, expressing faith in the Portuguese leadership that you can do this. That you can be a free country. That you haven't lost your revolution. It has taken a little detour, but you can work your way out of it. So, the positive outlook I think was extremely important.[63]

Subsequently, Soares and my father met many times at the American ambassador's residence. The stately neoclassical mansion occupies a prominent corner in a dignified part of town, but the two of them didn't meet in a grand dining room or opulent office. Instead, they convened in a room hidden away at the top of the building, on the fifth floor. Back then, the partially open-air area served as a laundry room, but my father liked to use it as a de facto meeting space for diplomatic engagement because of its beautiful views of the Tagus River. It was not much more than a small nook and required guests to climb multiple flights of stairs to reach it. It was later gussied up—enclosed, painted, and renamed the Crow's Nest. Today the room is on the register of historically important international places as designated by the State Department. My father and Soares spent many nights up there "working to advance democracy and human rights for the people of Portugal."[64]

In 2019, when the residence was renamed and dedicated as Casa Carlucci, the ambassador to Portugal, George Glass, referenced the Crow's Nest, the bond that formed there between my father and Soares, and the impact it had:

> During the *Verão Quente* of 1975, Frank Carlucci and Mário Soares met frequently in a tiny room we call the Crow's Nest—originally a laundry room—on the top floor of this house to exchange ideas on how to ensure that the Portuguese Revolution did not degenerate into a new dictatorship. This was a serious fear in Washington, so much so that Henry Kissinger had predicted that Mário Soares would share the fate of Alexander Kerensky, the head of the Russian Provisional Government that was swept away by the Bolsheviks. In August of 1975, Carlucci journeyed to Washington and took his case for backing Portugal's Democrats all the way to the White House, winning over President Ford and Secretary of State Kissinger.
>
> Washington then placed its bets on Portugal's democratic leaders, a decision vindicated by the defeat of the coup of November 25. When Mário Soares visited Washington in January of 1976, the talk with Kissinger had shifted to political and economic support for Portugal's constitutional transition. When Portugal's first constitutional government took office in July of 1976, with Soares at its head, Portugal's democratic future was secured. Carlucci

> then advocated successfully for economic support to stabilize Portugal's finances, and for military cooperation to reform Portugal's armed forces . . . I want to be crystal clear that my point is not to claim that Frank Carlucci and the United States brought democracy to Portugal. Mário Soares and Portugal's democratic parties did that. Frank Carlucci's contribution was to see the situation and Portugal's society clearly and convince Washington to stand with its friends.
>
> In 2006, Soares and Carlucci gave a joint interview to *Público* and were asked what would have happened if things went wrong, and Portugal had not taken the democratic path. Carlucci answered that the State Department would have fired him, and the hardliners in the administration would have rejoiced at having been proved right. Soares answered with the understatement, "*Para mim, teria sido um bocadinho pior.*" [For me, things would have been a little bit worse]. I think it is clear that Frank Carlucci understood that deeply, and therefore was ready to stake his reputation and career to stand with those who were risking even more to ensure the transition to democracy in Portugal.[65]

On November 25, 1975, there was an attempted Communist coup by left-wing activists. The response was swift and severe—the Portuguese Navy and Air Force remained loyal to the government, and within three days the coup was quelled. This coup spelled the end of the Communists, the military was purged of its leftists, and the armed forces were depoliticized. As Glass notes, my father was vindicated; he wrote back to Washington on November 26:

> Government forces are in control of [the] country with a few pockets of resistance remaining. Communists are laying low. Moderates have just about won a striking victory militarily. Pro-government forces, while stretched thin, are on top and have the momentum bred by success. Politically, we expect Popular Democrats, Socialists, and [the] prime minister to take [a] tougher stance on [the] Communist role in [the] government, and Costa Gomes [is] to resist expulsions of Communists from positions of influence. Moderates will exploit victory, but [a] lurch to [the] right will not take Portugal back to [a] pre-March 11, 1975 situation.[66]

Over the course of those crucial years, my father influenced Portugal's path to democracy in three major ways. First, he was active in the handling of the Azores crisis in the summer of 1975. A separatist movement there gained steam amid reports that Portugal would become communist. The Azores are extremely important to the United States because of a geostrategic military base at Lajes that is used for operations in the Middle East and as a pivotal staging ground for the United States and NATO.

His involvement with the situation began on April 2, 1975, when my father reported intelligence that armed actions were being prepared in the Azores by exiles from Spain.[67] My father advised the US position on the matter, suggesting that the US steer clear of supporting the independence movement. His recommendation was backed by Brent Scowcroft, Gerald Ford's national security advisor. His reasons were: (1) the idea that an uprising against leftists in the Azores would spread to mainland Portugal was "a pipedream"; (2) he only saw the downsides of US involvement: it could get back to Lisbon and could have cost the United

States access to Lajes Base; and (3) an armed coup in the Azores would only remind people of the mainland coup that resulted in a lurch to the left, potentially moving mainland Portugal closer to communism. Kissinger was initially keen on being more involved in the Azores; it was only in the summer of 1975 that my father's thinking won out and the US government's official position of neutrality on the matter was established.

Second, my father helped with the reorganization of the Portuguese military in 1976, which brought it into interoperability with NATO. Before then, Portuguese forces had not participated in NATO operations due to their numerous colonial wars raging overseas, and Portugal's military was also technologically behind many contemporaries. My father initially wanted to secure an aid package for the Portuguese military independently, but then realized Portugal instead needed to be more closely integrated into NATO's forces. He negotiated with General Eanes to provide funds to the Portuguese Army. This was a political move—a strong communist movement had taken hold in the Portuguese Navy and my father saw that if Portugal developed a strong Army, it would counterbalance a potential communist insurrection from within the Navy.

His third major contribution was a financial plan that would stabilize the weak and unpredictable Portuguese economy. In 1977, he crafted a financial plan that would transfer $550 million to Portugal to stabilize the economy, using loans distributed in three phases. The Portuguese economy had witnessed a 10 percent decline in GNP, near 15 percent unemployment, 20 percent inflation, and a 50 percent foreign reserve decline. The new democratic government might have fallen apart without this aid; at least this was what Kissinger said to justify this expenditure. Part of this loan was supported by the International Monetary Fund.[68]

Had Kissinger not been convinced otherwise, he would have supported the conservative elements of Portuguese society and potentially sparked a civil war. Instead, in 1976 Portugal adopted a democratic constitution and Soares led the Socialists to an electoral victory in 1976. Ever since then, Portugal has been a thriving democracy and NATO ally. My father was vindicated.

My father left his post on February 5, 1978. He had enjoyed his time there, but as he put it: "I was not sorry to contemplate leaving, however. I had become too much of a player on the scene. We needed somebody who was regarded more clinically." His legacy as an American hero continues to this day in Portugal, where the ambassador's residence and the American International School of Lisbon have been named after him. More specifically, his name is used to invoke the close historical ties between the two countries. When Ambassador George Edward Glass was appointed ambassador in 2017, he was told he had two very big pairs of shoes to fill, those of John Quincy Adams (who served as George Washington's ambassador to Portugal) and Frank Carlucci.[69]

Glass summarized my father's role in the preservation of democracy in Portugal in his speech during the dedication ceremony of Casa Carlucci:

> [I]n late 1974 Washington was nearly resigned to the idea that pro-communist forces would prevail in Portugal's internal political struggle. Pro-democracy parties were feared to be either too leftist, too weak (or both) to prevent this. Sent to Portugal in January of 1975, Ambassador Carlucci challenged this conclusion. He believed that, given the choice, the Portuguese people would vote to keep their nation anchored in Europe, NATO, and

> the transatlantic bond, and the result of the April 1975 Constituent Assembly elections proved it. As we all know, the parties that continue today as the Socialists, PSD, and CDS-PP combined to take 70 percent of the vote in that election. It was far from accepted in Washington, however, that the Portuguese Socialists, who had finished first, would steer developments in a democratic direction.
>
> Frank Carlucci left a tremendous—in a way intimidating—legacy for his successors to live up to. I feel that every day. His tenure here, and the American policy that he fought for, conceived, and implemented, are the best example we have of the friendship and trust we Americans have for our Portuguese friends. By naming this house in Frank Carlucci's honor, we remember that the strong bonds of friendship our countries share have been forged by leaders like Carlucci and Soares. We commit that it will continue to serve as space of dialogue, diplomacy, and democracy for generations to come.[70]

My father, in typical fashion, never took credit for helping pull the Portuguese back from the brink. In a 2009 interview with writer and historian Richard Norton Smith, he said,

> The Portuguese are very proud, justifiably so, of their move to a democratic system. Here is a tiny country that had a vast empire. Divested itself of that empire; overthrew a fascist dictatorship; went to the brink of communism, well it was all but taken over by the Communists; went to the brink of civil war; drew back and installed a fully functioning democracy which has survived to this day. All

> in the space of two years with very little bloodshed. It's a remarkable achievement and it's a case where the credit is due to the people themselves. They did it. So, they're justifiably proud of what they did.[71]

My father's friend and colleague John Garon went on to a long and distinguished career as a diplomat, and had this to say in summarizing his time in Portugal with my father:

> Serving at Embassy Lisbon under the direction of Frank C. Carlucci was the most professionally satisfying, and most productive time of my twenty-six years as an FSO. Serving FCC, and having known his wife Marcia, both of whom I came to consider friends, was a privilege and an honor.
>
> He was intellectually brilliant and had an uncanny talent to size up people and problems and determine a course of action instantly. He had an unusual ability to motivate people, to make his staff feel that we were playing an important role. Going to work each morning knowing that FCC was counting on me, if only to keep the lights on, was a pleasure. FCC had an understated charisma impossible to resist for those lucky enough to be in his inner orbit.
>
> FCC's career in the State Dept., HEW, OEO, CIA and DoD was the model to which any public servant could aspire, but never achieved. He was that rare person who could step in and out of his FSO career and political appointments with ease. Shy by temperament, FCC's shell was not easy to crack; he seemed ill at ease at functions that were not scripted, he did not suffer fools gladly, or

at all, and aimless blather bored him. One-on-one, FCC was a delightful interlocutor, a fount of knowledge on US domestic politics, and a sage advisor to any FSO seeking to serve his country.[72]

CHAPTER SIX

WORKING WASHINGTON

WHEN JIMMY CARTER WAS elected president of the United States, my father got a call from the State Department saying that Cyrus Vance, the new secretary of state, wanted him to be under secretary for administration. My father laughed. It would have made him the "principal advisor to the secretary and deputy secretary on matters relating to the allocation and use of Department of State resources (budget, physical property, and personnel), including planning, the day-to-day administration of the Department, and proposals for institutional reform and modernization."[73]

As a Republican, he knew the Democratic politicians would never allow him to get through the nomination process required for that job. Apparently, State Department officials had checked with the president. Carter liked my father and wanted to go ahead, but he also said: "I think you're going to have trouble."

Sure enough, there was opposition. So, my father continued in his role as ambassador until he received another phone call—this time from Admiral Stansfield Turner, who had been nominated director of Central Intelligence. He asked if my father would consider being his deputy. My father recalled Stan "as a very bright admiral who liked to break crockery and shake things up. He would surely be difficult to work with. But I had worked with CIA people in the past and found it interesting."

At that time, my father also felt that he had become too involved in the local elements of life in Portugal and that the United States now needed a more "clinical" ambassador. As a political appointee, he anticipated he was likely to be replaced by a Democrat anyway, with the change in administration.

I never heard much from my father directly about his time at the CIA, but I've learned from historical accounts and from personal records what his tenure there was like. For starters, Admiral Stansfield Turner was a controversial director. President Carter chose him in part because he knew Turner was a good axe man. The president wanted no less than drastic reform of the intelligence agencies, which had suffered a number of recent scandals, including Watergate. Aside from Watergate, alarm bells were going off as it became clear that American intelligence agencies were spying on citizens who were part of the antiwar movement or were suspected members of other dissident groups. Another scandal involved the numerous international assassination plots that came to light during this time. The United States Senate Select Committee to Study Governmental Operations with Respect to Intelligence Activities, or the "Church Committee," and its counterparts the United States House Permanent Select Committee on Intelligence (also known as the Pike Committee) and the

United States President's Commission on CIA Activities within the United States (also known as the Rockefeller Commission), were high-profile investigations that looked into these and other abuses of intelligence. It was during this time that the world also learned about MKUltra, a secret series of experiments on US citizens that used drugs and psychological torture as a part of interrogation techniques.

Turner came into the CIA with a mission to clean house, which he did by eliminating over eight hundred positions. The collective dismissals were known as "the Halloween massacre."[74] This dramatically reduced the clandestine side of the CIA, which helped to modernize the agency by moving the focus away from human intelligence and toward technical and signals intelligence. My father noted a particular shift in the culture of the CIA that occurred during his time working with Turner. The two of them brought young people up through the ranks and sought out their ideas and opinions. They also tried to bring coherence to departments within the CIA so it could work more efficiently with partner agencies. My father noted in an interview:

> I had worked with the agency throughout my Foreign Service career . . . I had a very good understanding of their activities on the ground. I saw no conflict between the State Department and the CIA although I spent a large portion of my time trying to prove that I was right . . .
>
> There's no question the culture was changing. They were traditionalists. The OSS types were fading out. Stan Turner . . . was very much a nontraditionalist. He liked to dive down and pull up the young people and make their voices heard. So, we did shake the place up. We said we're

> going to bring about closer relationships between the clandestine service and the analytical side. So, I think we began to change the culture considerably.

My father frequently reiterated that he was on the management side of the CIA, handling day-to-day affairs, and that he had little to do with what was happening on the intelligence side of things. My father enjoyed his time at the CIA overall, but later recalled that the amount of reading required was "quite challenging."

His time there also took place at the height of the Cold War. The Soviets were enemy No. 1, and their activities were top of mind for everyone involved in foreign policy in any way. Regardless of the truth of the matter, my father was the subject of more than a little suspicion. As he recalled:

> I had come in direct contact with the Soviet threat in Portugal. The Communists put out a book called *Dossier Carlucci's CIA*. It was about an inch thick. It had me doing everything from assassinating Moro the Italian prime minister to killing Lumumba to instigating the counter revolution in Brazil. They had me responsible for everything. So, I was very familiar with the kind of tactics they used.

My father did not have an in-depth knowledge of the Soviet military establishment when he started at the CIA, but he learned very quickly. "I certainly had no illusions on their system or what they were up to or what their goals were . . . In retrospect, I think our judgements on the size and capabilities of the [Soviet] military were quite accurate. What we did not anticipate was the economic weaknesses that would lead to the collapse . . ."

Tensions were also running high in the Middle East. My father was involved in the planning of Desert I, one phase of the attempt to rescue fifty-two Americans who were taken hostage at the American embassy in Tehran in November of 1979 (the entire extraction was entitled Operation Eagle Claw). The idea was that once the hostages left the building, the Desert I plan would ensure there were US operatives along the roads to safeguard the transit of hostages to the airport, where they would be removed by helicopter. As he notes, my father was in National Security Advisor Zbigniew Brzezinski's office when the decision was made to move forward with the rescue attempt. This was done against the counsel of Secretary of State Cy Vance, who virulently opposed the plan.

The rescue operation was in fact unsuccessful—the hostages would have to wait until January 20, 1981, to be released. Vance resigned in outrage over the operation, about which my father recalled, "I thought that was a shame, since Cy Vance was a first-rate man and a good secretary of state." He was also of the opinion that "the failed rescue mission probably cost [Carter] the presidency. At least it hurt him badly."

The night the decision was made to move forward with the operation, my dad went right from the White House to George Washington University Hospital for my birth. Luckily, I wasn't quick about making my appearance, so he was able to make it in time.

My parents had been quite surprised to learn of my impending arrival. They had been enjoying settling back into political and social life in Washington and were not entirely prepared for a newborn and the disruption it would bring to their lifestyle, since by this point my half brother and sister were already launched into their own lives.

When my parents had returned from Portugal in 1978, they had bought a home in the leafy DC suburb of McLean, Virginia. Despite my father's outward signs of success, they still needed a loan from my grandfather (Frank Carlucci II) to make the down payment. I'm sure that even if he didn't say it aloud, my grandfather likely mumbled the old line about "Shoulda been a businessman . . ."

My father's life was about to change drastically in more ways than one.

Ronald Reagan became president on January 20, 1981. In a private meeting with my father, Cap Weinberger revealed that he was going to be named secretary of defense and he wanted my father to serve as his deputy. Initially Dad refused, saying that he was flat broke and couldn't afford to stay in government. But his sense of duty won the day, as it always did.

It wasn't smooth sailing from there, though. My father ran into trouble during the confirmation process from right-wing Senator Jesse Helms from North Carolina. Helms managed to convince three or four senators to join his opposition, including Orrin Hatch, who later called my father to apologize. This held up the nomination process by about three months—and it took an intervention by the president for Helms to back down.

Once in office, my father found being deputy secretary of defense "a difficult but pleasant job. I had to learn all the weapon systems, the technical terms and manage the acquisition process. I also had to cope with fierce infighting and lobbying."

My father worked closely with Cap Weinberger, assuming responsibility for the day-to-day management of the Pentagon. He and Weinberger grew very close.

Weinberger and my father developed a good division of labor. As he recalled, "Cap liked the foreign affairs aspect of the job

My great-grandfather, Frank Carlucci I, who came to Scranton, Pennsylvania, from Santomenna in Salerno, Italy.

My grandfather, Frank Carlucci II, with my father in 1933.

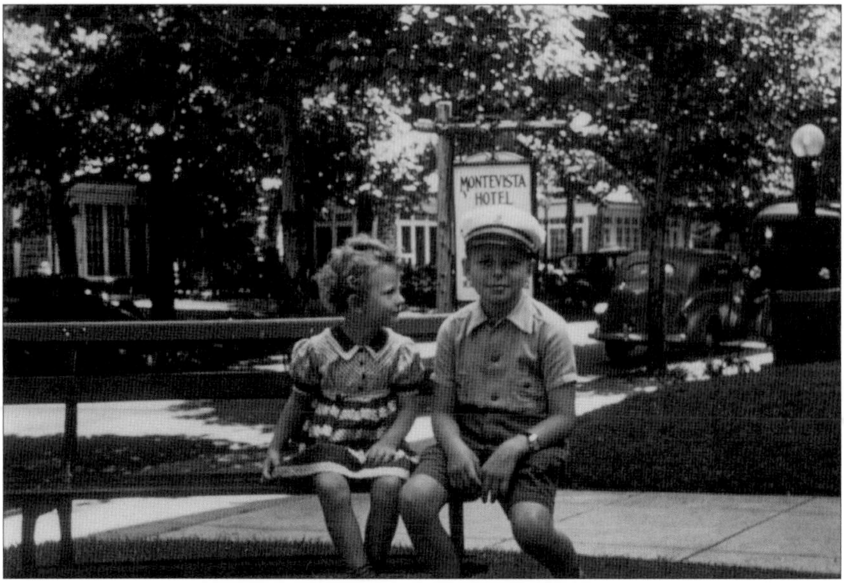

My father with his only sibling, Joan, in 1939.

My father (back row, center) was a star on the wrestling team of his prep school in Wilkes-Barre, Pennsylvania, in 1948.

My father served in the Navy, starting in 1952, as a first lieutenant on a destroyer escort based out of Seattle.

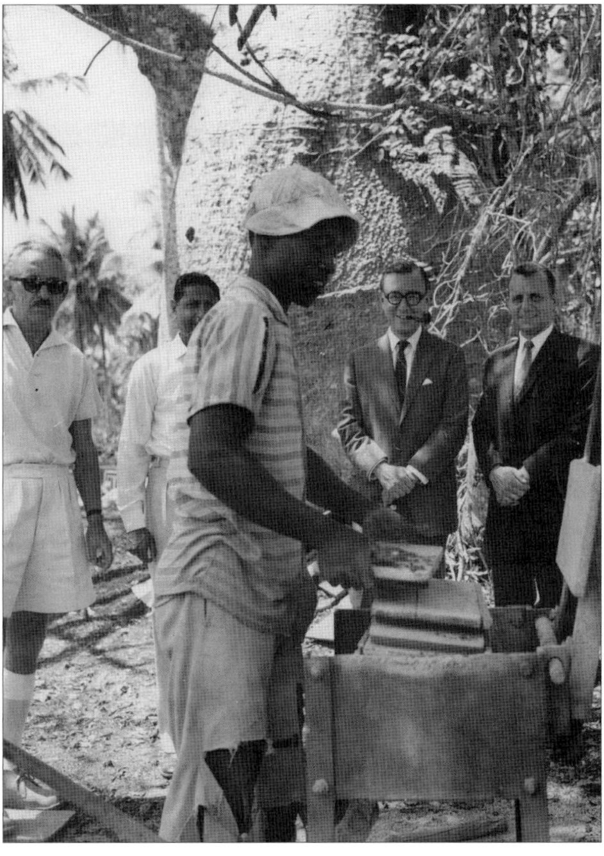

Ambassador William Leonhart and my father in Zanzibar in 1964. The two of them worked relentlessly to secure a robust US presence in the area.

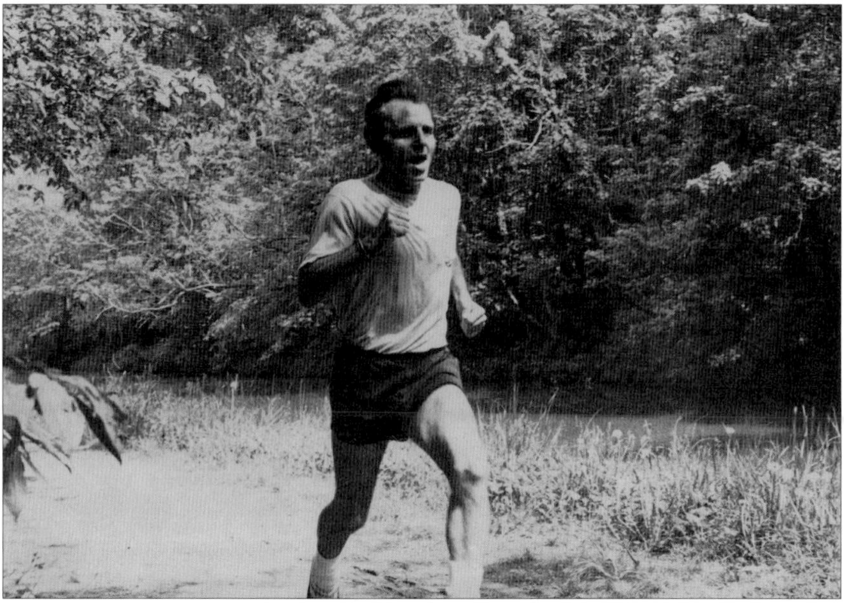

Throughout his time in Washington, DC, my father exercised on the Chesapeake & Ohio ("C&O") Canal.

My father at the Office of Economic Opportunity in 1971. (White House official)

My brother, Frank "Chip" Carlucci IV, with our father in 1971. (White House official)

In the aftermath of Hurricane Agnes in 1972, my father returned to his hometown of Wilkes-Barre, Pennsylvania, with President Richard Nixon to spearhead relief efforts.

President Gerald Ford was "an extraordinary man" according to my father. He regularly worked with President Ford during his time as undersecretary of the Department of Health, Education, and Welfare. (1974)

Socialist Foreign Minister Mário Soares was my father's key ally in Portugal and would later go on to serve as prime minister of Portugal from 1976 to 1978. (Jorge Paula, 1975)

My father and my mother, Marcia Myers Carlucci, right after their 1976 wedding in Portugal.

Chip and my father on my father's birthday, complete with a tennis-themed cake, in Lisbon, Portugal. (1976)

My father, Director of Central Intelligence Stansfield Turner, and President Jimmy Carter in the Oval Office. (White House official, 1978)

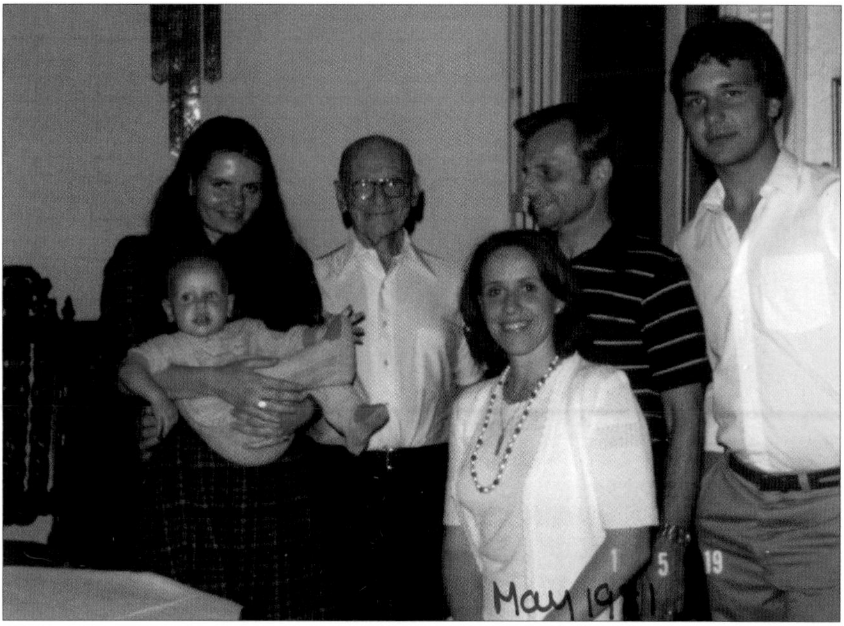

My sister, Karen Carlucci Romano, holding me. Next to us are my grandfather, my father, Chip, and my mother. (1981)

My father on a 1982 visit to the headquarters of the 94th Tactical Air Command.

My father and I starting some early tennis instruction. (1982)

My father and Caspar Weinberger chatting with me at the Secretary of Defense Christmas Party in 1984.

President Reagan meets with former President Nixon and my father to discuss China. (Howard Baker, 1986)

My father working with President Reagan. When my father later resigned as secretary of defense, Reagan wrote of his "significant accomplishments." (White House official, 1987)

Caspar Weinberger, President Ronald Reagan, my father, and Colin Powell at the official announcement of my father as new secretary of defense. (White House official, 1987)

My father inspecting the troops in 1987.

Chief of Staff Howard Baker shows my father the votes to confirm him as secretary of defense while Deputy Chief of Staff Kenneth Duberstein looks on. (1988)

The meeting of the Russians and the Americans in 1988. Soviet Defense Minister Dmitry Yazov and my father sit at the center of the table.

Me, my father, Minister Yazov, and various family members and representatives on our 1990 trip to Moscow.

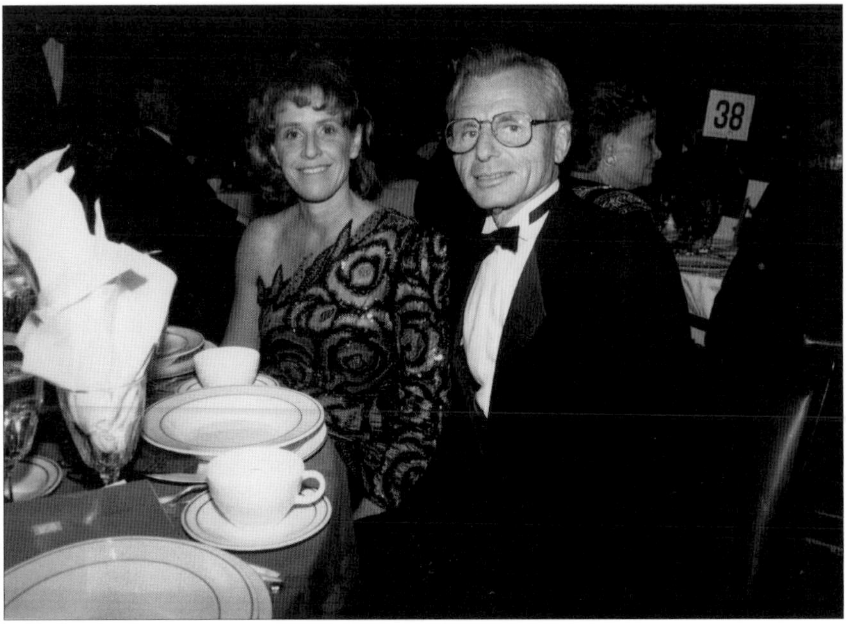

My mother and father out on the town.

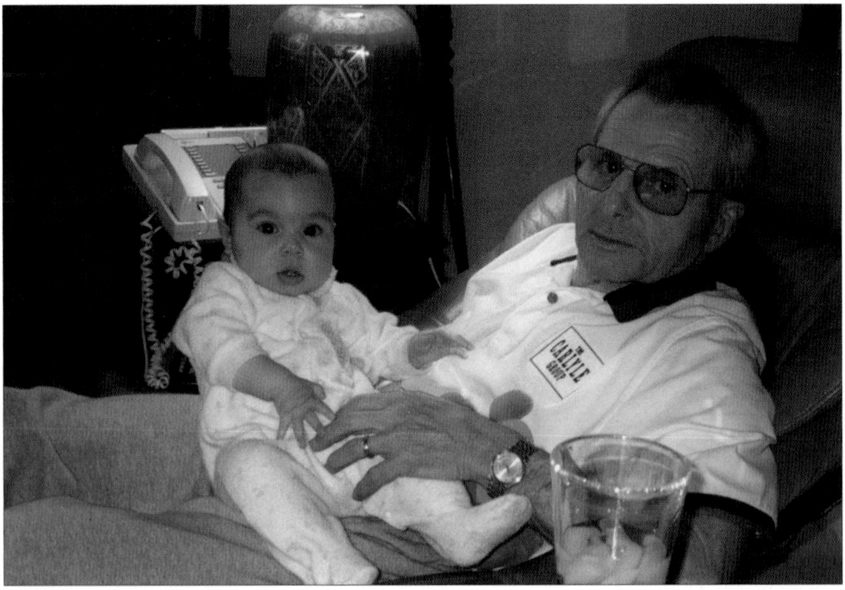

My father in his role as "Bumpa" with my niece, Marina, in 2000.

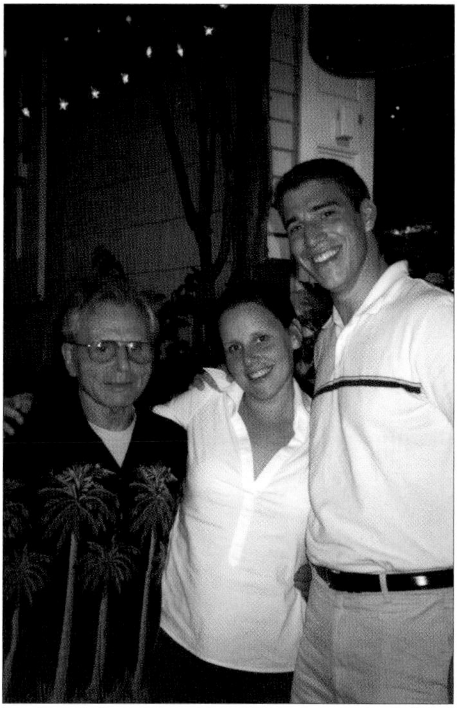

My father, me, and my husband, Josh Weed, on a 2006 trip to St. Maarten.

My mother and father attended the Pentagon promotion ceremony for my husband, Lt. Col. Joshua Weed, in 2006.

My daughter Amelia, Josh, me, my mother, and my father at the Frank C. Carlucci American International School on our 2011 trip to Portugal.

and enjoyed traveling. I focused on the budget and procurement, seeing that our forces were well supplied, modernized, and ready."

Budget and procurement were topics that were prone to igniting fierce infighting and lobbying. He created the Defense Resources Board and proposed what ended up being called the "Carlucci Initiatives" to bring more accountability and logic into the defense procurement process. These thirty-two recommendations were made to reduce costs and improve the acquisition process throughout the Department of Defense—no small task given that the Reagan administration oversaw the most expensive peacetime expansion of the US military in history, with the DoD budget exploding from $142 billion in 1980 to $286 billion in 1985.[75] My father's goals were to completely overhaul the procurement process to keep costs down, shorten the time it took for procurement, and find creative solutions to issues like the question of which military equipment to invest in, tried-and-true performers or cutting-edge technologies.

My father's stint in the CIA had definitely left a mark on the way he did things. He recalled a time when there was a leak that had obviously come directly from a closed-door meeting my father had held. He was determined to catch the leaker and recalled,

> I conducted an investigation. I used a polygraph, which had never been used in the Department of Defense, but had been used frequently in the CIA. I took the first polygraph and was followed by all the members of the Joint Chiefs. We found out who the leaker was, but before I could take any action, I received a phone call from his senator, who happened to be chairman of our committee. He told me not to take any action. At the same time, the

> lawyers came in and said I could not take any action on the basis of a polygraph. It would never stand up in a court of law. So, I had to back down, accepting how difficult it is to fire a government servant.

The massive buildup of federal defense spending inevitably made headlines for multiple instances of fraud, corruption, mismanagement, and waste by DoD and defense firms, famously including the $435 hammer, the $640 toilet seat, and $7,600 coffee makers.[76] My father admitted, "It's true we spent a lot of money. It's also true that there were some mistakes such as expensive toilet seats and hammers." Nonetheless, my father supported the buildup of the military. He described his working relationship with the president, the secretary of state, and the director of the OMB with this episode:

> Ronald Reagan had said during his campaign, and he continued to say, that we would only negotiate from a position of strength. The first step was to rebuild our military. Whenever OMB Director David Stockman stood in the way, Cap would steamroll him by going directly to the president, who uniformly supported us. I can remember one meeting we had in Los Angeles where Cap and David Stockman were briefing the president. I had worked with the Army to develop a graph. It showed a big muscular soldier entitled "Ronald Reagan soldier" and a little scrawny soldier entitled "Stockman soldier." Stockman was absolutely livid, but the tactic worked, and the president sided with us on the budget.

My father and Weinberger made a good team, with Weinberger taking strong positions externally and my father working behind the scenes to negotiate. My father understood the president's priorities and his style, though you did not have to be an insider to do so: Reagan often publicly stated that he wanted no new taxes and the best military in the world. There was one event with which my father had firsthand involvement that illustrates the change in attitude toward the military that occurred with the transfer of power from President Carter to Reagan. As my father recalled:

> I was in my office one day and my then military assistant, General Colin Powell, came in and said "Frank, I've got a confession to make."
>
> I said, "What's that?"
>
> "I've been holding on my desk a Congressional Medal of Honor Award to a man named Sergeant Benavides."
>
> "Why have you been holding it?"
>
> "Because it was well known that President Carter would not grant personally any medals of honor for Vietnam service."
>
> I said, "Let me read it."
>
> It related incredible acts of heroism on the part of Sergeant Benavides. I took it immediately into Cap's office. I said, "Cap you're going to see the president in a few minutes on another matter—but read this."
>
> Cap read it and said, "My goodness, the president will love this."
>
> He took it to the president, whose first question was: "How soon can I come over to the Pentagon to present

it?" He then called twice more to ask when we were going to have the ceremony ready.

President Reagan came over and made the presentation at the outset of his administration and the effects throughout the military were electric. They knew they had somebody who understood and cared for them, and who would take the time to stand with them.

My father and General Colin Powell had crossed paths earlier, when Powell was a young White House fellow and my father was at OMB. They got to know each other better at the Pentagon in the early 1980s, when Powell became my father's military assistant. Their friendship would last the rest of my father's life, and Powell would be one of the eulogizers at my father's funeral in 2018. In a sad twist of fate, I had the extraordinary opportunity to interview Powell just weeks before he passed away in 2021. We sat in his office in his home in McLean, Virginia, as he jokingly shared stories of how my father was determined to "derail" Powell's career; it seemed whenever Powell was getting settled into a role, my father was appointed to a new position where he would then call upon Powell to join him. My father trusted Colin Powell implicitly, his judgment, his good sense, his morals.

Powell and Weinberger: these were two of the colleagues who shaped my father's professional life. When he spoke at my father's funeral, Powell said the following about him, which I feel reflects the special attitude that *both* men had toward their careers and toward the people with whom they worked: "Always willing to give or share the credit with others. A man who had our love and respect, who we would follow anywhere . . . A servant without any pretensions or expectation of reward: the opportunity to serve again was the only reward he sought." Despite politics being maligned as dirty, selfish work, it's actually hard to make a lasting impact or leave a legacy in Washington without having—and being—a good mentor.

Weinberger and my father played to each other's strengths, and my father stepped in when Weinberger's patience ran thin. For instance, Weinberger had no tolerance for arguing with OMB, where he had once been director. Basically, OMB would only speak with my father. On the Hill, Weinberger was the ultimate stonewall. He would take a position and repeat it over and over. This generated a lot of frustration, but it worked. From time to time, members of Congress would come to my father and make a plea for him to take a certain action that Weinberger opposed. My father would then quietly work with Weinberger to develop a modified position. He was helped greatly in this effort by William "Will" Taft—who was general counsel of the Department of Defense and a longtime friend of Cap's—and by Colin Powell, whom Weinberger made his military assistant soon after my father left the Department of Defense.

After two years, my father reminded Weinberger of his promise to stay only that long. My father told him, "We have a young daughter, and I have to think about her future as well as my son's education. I'm in my fifties, so I've got to put something aside." Weinberger offered that he would happily lend my father the money if he would stay on. My father declined the generous offer.

With two older children, one a son in college, and me now on the scene, my father felt the pressure to make some money. He was taking out loans to keep Chip in college. At the time, he was earning $60,000 per year (and a government pension that would amount to $30,000 per year) and lamented that the government couldn't pay enough to keep people once they had gained the experience they needed.

Working together as secretary of defense and deputy secretary, my father and Weinberger came to understand each other well. In a 1989 interview my father said of him:

> I think Cap Weinberger is a superb human being. He was as fine, decent, and dedicated a secretary as you will ever find. He has an element of inflexibility in him; there's no question about that. The only way to get around that, I found, was to sit down quietly with him and work through the issues, and, over a period of time, to get him to change. Confrontation with Cap does not work. He is an extraordinarily bright and talented individual who holds atrociously long staff meetings, I told him that many times . . . He is thoroughly considerate; the kind of man who insists that his secretaries are invited to his dinners when he is traveling; he goes back in the airplane to make sure they are in good shape. He was always calling me and asking how I was . . . He is just a wonderful human being to work with. He defends what he believes in . . . Like everybody, he is sensitive to criticism, but he plunges ahead.[77]

For his part, Weinberger said of my father,

> He brought a sharp and searching mind, which was ready to challenge pat assumptions and burrow for the truth. He brought loyalty and immense personal integrity. He brought an extraordinary capacity for hard work. He is something of a hero among civil servants and, like all of

us, they sorely need heroes. Maybe more than the rest of us because they make such an easy target for attack. Frank has always impressed upon me the value of the men and women who have spent their professional lives working for the government. Their accumulated knowledge, their loyalty to the nation they serve, get far too little recognition, and far too often, far too little trust."[78]

As he was deciding to leave government employment, my father weighed his private sector options. The transition was something that he had seen others struggle with, so he reached out to his colleagues who had been through it. Donald Rumsfeld, who served on the board of Sears, connected him with Rod Hills, who was then the CEO designate for Sears World Trade. Sears World Trade was a startup venture, essentially a trading company within the larger retail giant. My father was named vice chairman of Sears World Trade, which unfortunately hired staff faster than they made money, souring relations between Sears and Sears World Trade. Shortly after he joined, Sears decided to remove the chairman of Sears World Trade and name my father as the new chairman. Although Sears was now making money at a good pace, the new CEO of Sears, Ed Brennan, called my father in early 1986 and told him the parent company had decided to shutter Sears World Trade. My father wound up having to let many good people go as a result. Reflecting on the failures of Sears World Trade, he noted:

> Part of the idea was that we could buy goods cheaper, because Sears had buying power overseas, and sell them in the United States; and we could bundle exports from various US companies and get economies of scale that way and export overseas. There were a couple of things wrong with that philosophy, as it later turned out. One is that it was not easy to leverage off of Sears' buying power because Sears was a great big bureaucracy and Sears buyers weren't particularly interested in Sears World Trade. It didn't help their bonus. We were never able to fully exploit the Sears buying power. Secondly, on the exporting side, we ran headlong into a very strong dollar. Exports were pretty expensive. We made some mistakes on our own too. We created a large infrastructure before we had the business to support that infrastructure.
>
> We existed for a couple of years and never really got to the break-even point, but we were lost in the rounding for Sears Roebuck . . . When Ed Brennan became CEO of Sears, it became pretty obvious to me that Sears World Trade's days were numbered because Ed Brennan really wanted to go back to traditional merchandising. He was a second-generation Sears person and very much oriented towards the domestic operations of Sears and not very interested in international activities.[79]

One day while my father was in the process of dismantling Sears World Trade, he went out to lunch at the Willard Hotel, and the waiter told him he had an urgent call from Donald "Don" Regan, chief of staff for President Reagan. Regan asked my father to come in and meet with the president. He was instructed to slip in the back way through the Treasury entrance and meet in the basement of the White House. Just the three of them met—President Reagan, Donald Regan, and my father. The president came to the point rather quickly. He wanted my father to be his new national security advisor. He had fired the previous one, along with Colonel Oliver North. Both were involved in the Iran-Contra affair and Reagan's presidency was under attack as a result.

The president didn't say he wanted my father because of his strong background or his above-average intelligence. Reagan said he wanted him because he was the only person George Shultz and Cap Weinberger could agree on. "Hardly a clarion call, but that was Ronald Reagan," my father wrote in his memoirs later. "I described to him what I thought my strong points and weak points were. I told him he was not getting a brilliant strategic thinker, but he was getting somebody who knew how to run things. He said fine. I agreed to take the job starting in January; this was in November." To me, this quote is my dad in a nutshell! He never overestimated his intelligence, but he also never underestimated his ability to find a way to get things done.

My father was the national security advisor from January 1, 1986, to November 1987. Robert Gates, who was then deputy director of the CIA and later secretary of defense (2006 to 2011), described my father's contribution in the following terms:

> With Frank's reputation for integrity, courage, and effective leadership of complex government enterprises, it was no surprise President Reagan turned to him in the aftermath of the Iran-Contra scandal to right the national security ship—the National Security Council and its staff

> and White House relationships with the Departments of State and Defense, as well as [the] CIA. With the help of another experienced, adept leader as his deputy—then Lieutenant General Colin Powell—Frank Carlucci played a big role in the significant foreign policy achievements of the last two years of the Reagan presidency.[80]

One of my father's first actions as national security advisor was to get Colin Powell on board:

> My first move was to abolish the double deputy structure that had been in place, create a single deputy slot and ask Colin Powell to fill it. It took a call directly from the president, which I programmed, to persuade Colin to come back from a choice military assignment in Germany, but he did, and he took over very quickly. I told Colin he could attend all my meetings with the president.

Once instated as the NSA, my father spent a great deal of time going through arms control negotiations that had been stalled. He also dramatically reworked the organizational structure of the National Security Council. As his comments above reveal, he had two deputies at first and then he decided he needed only one: Colin Powell. My father said this was probably the best career move he ever made.

At the time, Colin Powell was not so happy about being called upon to be deputy national security advisor. In a conversation in October of 2021, Powell recalled the situation when my father called to convince him to return to Washington, DC, to work for him, and what transpired between them before and after:

I had been selected to be a White House fellow and I was being interviewed to see where I would spend my fellowship year. Frank Carlucci was deputy director of OMB and my last interviewer. I wanted to be posted to OMB because it would give me a broader view of government but also because I might work with Mr. Carlucci . . . However shortly after I got the OMB assignment, Frank moved to the Department of Health, Education and Welfare along with Cap Weinberger, the OMB director who was the new secretary of HEW. . . The years passed. I didn't see Frank or Cap until January 1981 when they came to the Defense Department as secretary and deputy secretary in the Reagan administration. I was in the Pentagon serving as the military assistant to the Deputy Secretary Graham Claytor. I was anxious to return to the Army but Frank, remembering me, had a different idea. He arranged for me to stay on awhile as his military assistant. I don't recall him asking me if I wanted to. I did it with pleasure and learned a lot from him in the months we were together. However, I didn't realize that part of my duty was to be two-year-old Kristin's babysitter when he occasionally brought her to the office if he had to work on a Saturday. Frank was definitely a family man, a Marcia man. Secretary Weinberger wanted to have a daily staff meeting at 8 a.m. Marcia said he couldn't be there that early, so the staff meeting started at 8:30.

After several months I persuaded Frank to release me, and I went back to the Army for the next two years. I was then suddenly ordered back to the Pentagon to serve as Secretary Weinberger's military assistant. I knew Frank was behind it all because he left shortly thereafter for private life.

After a couple of terrific years with Cap, the Army selected me to command an infantry division in Germany. I was overjoyed. Alas, Cap wanted me to stay another year and General John Wickham, the Army chief of staff, concurred. Mr. Weinberger comforted me that evening by saying with a smile that the Army would give me command of a corps in a year that had two divisions in it. See? Even better.

In the July of the next year, 1986, I took command of the Fifth Corps with headquarters in Frankfurt. One afternoon six months later I got a call from Frank. The Iran-Contra scandal was raging, and he had just been selected to be the new national security advisor. I foolishly thought he was calling just to inform me about his new job. How nice! I congratulated him. He immediately pocketed that and said he wanted me to return to Washington as his deputy. I protested. Frank! Not again. My fellow officers would write me off if I simply walked away from this command. Frank said it was that important. I had only one card to play. "Frank, if it is that important shouldn't the president call me?" One hour later the phone rang in the kitchen. It was a short conversation with the president. You know the rest of the story. I said "Yes, sir," and [my wife] Alma started packing the next day . . .

We had similar thinking about leadership. He had a lot of exercise in leadership, but by then I had been a very senior general and I knew a lot about leadership as I saw it, too. And we fired almost everybody who was in that office . . . I said, "Frank, you already have two other deputies." I said, "I'm not coming there if there are three deputies. I'm either your deputy or I'm not, that's my style,

> but you can't have three deputies." And he said, "Okay, go fire the other two . . ."
>
> The president thought the world of him. I thought the world of him. He gave me a great deal of latitude since I was his only deputy. He had confidence in me and . . . I had more confidence in him. I learned a lot from him, and I think he learned a bit from me, but we were a good team.[81]

While he and Powell were slimming down the staff, my father also eliminated the separate office of Political-Military Affairs. In his view, the whole National Security Council (NSC) was political-military affairs, and by giving that title its own distinction, it gave free rein to the individual in that office to act on their own accord. Oliver North had previously held the job, which was evidence of this fact. North was given free rein "to go hunting" and he went out looking for problems to solve single-handedly—and got himself into lots of trouble doing so.

In the end, my father estimates he fired about 65 percent of the staff at the NSC (firing people who he deemed redundant or unnecessary was clearly a recurring theme in my father's professional life). Ultimately, the NSC is composed of people borrowed from other agencies, so saying he fired 65 percent of the NSC staff is a bit dramatic. It's likely most returned to their primary agencies. The NSC is probably the most volatile body within the White House—it varies from administration to administration, so fluctuations of staff levels are quite normal. Nevertheless, "Vice President George Bush called me in and told me that the president was getting worried that I was firing too many people. At Bush's suggestion, I sent a handwritten note to the president saying I thought restructuring the NSC was essential and not to worry, that it would come out all right. And indeed, it did."

My father sometimes butted heads with George Shultz, who had a general distrust of any NSC advisor. As my father recalled:

> I told him I would keep him fully informed but that I was working for the president, not for him. George did not want me to chair meetings, travel, or meet with ambassadors. I said none of this was acceptable, that I didn't come back to government to be an executive secretary. I would get my oar in on policy, but I would let the agency heads have their say first. I would not block access to the president. George and I did some further sparring but fundamentally we worked toward the same goal.

As national security advisor, my father saw the president practically every day to brief him on what was happening with different agencies. He recalled,

> He was always very gracious, except for one time. We went to Canada to meet with Prime Minister Mulroney, whom Reagan really liked. The two of them would swap Irish jokes on and on. Reagan said to me as he drove up, "Be nice to the Canadians." We were having lunch at Mulroney's house and Mulroney's chief of staff and I were arguing across the table.
>
> Mulroney saw that and said, "Perhaps you would like to huddle with your staff, Mr. President?" So, we went to a sitting room. I sat on one side of the president and George Shultz sat on the other. George and I started to argue. I

was holding to a position that various agencies had taken, which was a harder line than George wanted.

Finally, Reagan said, "I told you to be nice to the Canadians. Do it!"

I left and went back to Derek Burney, Mulroney's chief of staff, and said, "Derek would you repeat your position to me because it's now ours!" That was the only time Reagan ever had a harsh word for me. He was always very supportive.

Later, one of my father's missions was to extricate Reagan from the Iran-Contra affair. "It was harder than I had thought," he said.

I can remember briefing him at an economic conference in Venice, just prior to a press conference, and saying, "The first question will be on Iran-Contra, and I suggest you say we're here to discuss economics. You've said enough about Iran-Contra and let's get on with the economic questions." I was hopeful he would do that. Sure enough, the first question was from Helen Thomas, one of the old-line reporters, a tough lady, and it was on Iran-Contra. Reagan gave that circular explanation again. It looked like only the passage of time would solve that problem. I think probably to his dying day President Reagan did not believe he traded arms for hostages. History will have to make a judgment on that.

Iran-Contra was Reagan's Watergate—a major scandal and a black mark on his presidency forever. Senior officials had been selling arms to Iran—despite the arms embargo—to fund the Contras, right-wing rebels in Nicaragua backed by the United States. Funding the Contras was prohibited by Congress, and Carter had placed an arms embargo on Iran after the Iran hostage crisis. When this became public knowledge, it grew into a huge political scandal. Reagan didn't address the American people for three months. (Later in his life he frequently expressed his regrets over how this situation unfolded. But this was far after the fact.) John Poindexter, the previous NSA, resigned, and Reagan fired Oliver North. North had hidden or destroyed vital documents with the assistance of his secretary, Fawn Hall, who was also fired (by my father and Colin Powell).

My father remembered Reagan as

> both easy and difficult to work for. Easy because he was accessible, had certain principles that we all understood, and put great faith and responsibility in his subordinates. In fact, when Colin and I came out of the first briefing we had with him, I said to Colin that I didn't know we had signed on to run the world. We went back to my office. I told Colin that we were going to have to adopt a different style. We would have to figure out what Ronald Reagan would do because we couldn't get clear answers from him, and we couldn't let the world know that he didn't go into much depth on many of the subjects. I was surprised when I read his handwritten notes, which were published after his death, to see how much of what we had told him he had absorbed. He just didn't react and didn't like giving clear instructions or engaging in confrontation. But he had a magnificent ability for meeting with people, hearing their

complaints, not letting his pockets be picked, and exuding charm. We also knew that whenever we got into trouble, we could make up the cue cards and put him on television and he could sway the day. He could bring people along like nobody I've ever known. In a broad sense, Jimmy Carter would dive into all the details and frequently not come out in the right place. Ronald Reagan seemed to absorb or communicate few of the details, but his instincts invariably brought him to the right place.

Ronald Reagan also didn't like confrontation. As I remember it, Don Regan, his chief of staff, and I were having breakfast and I said, "Don, has anybody talked to you about Howard Baker replacing you?"

He said, "No."

I said, "Well the rumors are all over town."

At about 2 p.m. that afternoon, I got a call from Bob Tuthill, the chief of White House personnel. "Frank," he said, "it's on CNN that Howard Baker is replacing Don Regan."

I said, "Why are you calling me?"

"Because you're the next highest-ranking person in the White House."

"Well, all right I'll see what I can do."

So, I called the president up in his quarters and I told him this rumor was out. I asked, "Have you said anything to Don, Mr. President?"

"Uh oh," came his reply.

I said, "Well, let me see what I can do."

So, I went down to Don Regan's office, tossed out a *New York Times* reporter and told Don that the rumor that had been mentioned that morning was in fact true. Regan blew his stack.

So, I went back and called the president again. I said, "Mr. President, there is no avoiding this. You've got to talk to Don."

I got back to Don's office just as the phone was ringing and he was refusing to answer it. I can remember saying, "For Christ's sake Don, he's the president of the United States. Answer the phone!"

He did and it was a very brief phone call. That's when he dictated his one sentence letter: "I hereby resign as your chief of staff."

❋❋❋

The country was still in the midst of the Cold War. Reagan was categorically opposed to nuclear weapons and the idea of mutually assured destruction (MAD) that some of his predecessors had supported. In the March 23, 1983, speech in which he announced the Strategic Defense Initiative (SDI) to the American people, Reagan described MAD as "a sad commentary on the human condition" and added that he would endeavor "to save lives rather than avenge them."[82] The SDI was intended to act as a shield from nuclear attack, ending the Cold War by making nuclear war impossible. However, critics expressed disbelief that such a shield could be technologically achieved and maintained, leading critics to dub SDI the "Star Wars program" in part due to the fantasy nature of the technology it proposed and the use of lasers. Ultimately, the SDI program never was implemented, and, in hindsight, many top scientists concluded that the technology was still a decade away from being feasible. Although SDI had the potential to disrupt the fragile balance of arms in the Cold War, it did cause enough of a panic to provide Reagan with some necessary leverage in the Soviet Union, which at the time was falling apart internally. As my father recalled, "Many Americans were skeptical about SDI. Gorbachev wasn't. It became a virtual obsession with him. He saw it as seriously diminishing the USSR's strategic capability."

President Reagan requested that my father join the October 1986 delegation to negotiate the Intermediate-Range Nuclear Forces (INF) Treaty with the Soviet Union. The INF Treaty was an effort to eliminate all intermediate and short-ranged ground-based missiles and launchers from Europe, and it was widely regarded at that time as the most significant nuclear arms agreement in history.[83]

In the meeting, Mikhail Gorbachev described the problems the Soviets had with SDI, and he waited for a response from George Shultz. In his memoirs, my father recalls the confrontation:

Shultz said, "SDI is the president's program. I'll let Frank answer."

So, my father said, "Mr. Secretary-General, what you have just said is unacceptable to our president. He is not going to compromise SDI."

With that, Gorbachev threw down his pencil and said, "Then we won't have a summit."

My father recalled, "George, bless his heart, said, 'Fine, there will be no summit.'" That's why the summit was postponed from October to December.

When Reagan secured Soviet agreement on the INF Treaty on December 8, 1987, several prominent fellow Republicans publicly objected—including most notably former President Nixon. Presumably to quell the public disagreement, my father suggested bringing Nixon into the White House for a private meeting. Reagan agreed. They snuck him in via helicopter on the South Lawn. My father went out to the helicopter to meet him and took him directly to the White House elevators and up to Ronald Reagan's study. It was likely the first, and possibly the last, time Nixon was in the White House after leaving in disgrace. My father, Nixon, Reagan, and Reagan's new chief of staff, Howard Baker, met in private for an hour and a half to discuss the INF Treaty. Nixon did most of the talking, with Reagan listening attentively.[84]

As my father recollected in an interview:

> The president had a fascination with the Soviet Union. While the speech writers liked to put in "evil empire" and those kinds of things, he really had a deep interest in two things: freedom of religion in the Soviet Union and human rights. Finally, when I got to the NSC, there was a lady named Suzanne Massey who was a social anthropologist from Harvard who was the only outsider I could find that got in to see the president alone. She would go in and talk to him about the Soviet Union. I finally said to the president, "Look, Mr. President, I can't function as your national security advisor unless I know what's going on here."
>
> He said, "Fine, well you can sit in." So, I sat in and it was a very, perfectly proper, very cordial relationship that they had. She had a lot of impact on the president. They didn't talk much about geopolitics. They talked a lot about the social issues in the Soviet Union.

The president also used to carry around with him names of Soviet dissidents who'd been imprisoned. Where he got them, I don't know. Whenever George Shultz would go over there, he'd give George some names and say, "I'd like you to get this person or that person out."

Once we got the arms control decisions in place, there remained the question of conditioning the president to negotiations which we knew were coming. George Shultz had done a wonderful job, which he describes in his book, of conditioning the president for negotiations and then saying, "We're going to enter into negotiations. These are your choices. Do you want to do this?"

And Ronald Reagan, here's where he deserves real credit because his constituency was not terribly supportive, said, "Yes, we are going to negotiate with the Soviet Union . . ." I went to the president with a list of names. I can remember I mentioned Brzezinski he liked, Richard Pearl he liked, Kissinger he was not terribly keen to see, but the name that hit the jackpot was the first one I mentioned: Richard Nixon.

I said, "Why don't we start with him?" And I'm not sure this has come out to this day, but we smuggled Richard Nixon back into the White House. It was the first time he was in since he left the White House in disgrace, maybe the only time, I'm not sure. We flew him by helicopter to the back lawn and I met him right at the door of the White House basement entrance and I took him up to Ronald Reagan's study on the third floor of the White House. Just Richard Nixon, Ronald Reagan, Howard Baker, and me. Nixon and Reagan discussed the Soviet Union for I'd say, about an hour and a quarter, maybe two hours. Obviously a fascinating discussion. Nixon doing most of the talking, Reagan listening. And that's how we kicked off the preparations for the negotiations.

❋❋❋

My father had found his place, it seemed, and not just at work. I was three when my parents decided they had outgrown their first home in Northern Virginia. They bought a 1970s contemporary wood-framed house not far from the previous one. It had more space, plus a pool and a tennis court, to the delight of my exercise-loving parents. The home became a sanctuary for my dad, and an important place for my family to gather over the years.

During holidays in those early years at the house, we would all gather, and my father relished his role as the patriarch. He would sit at the end of our long dining room table at holidays, and he always said the prayer at dinners. Beforehand he would sit quietly as everyone else rushed around, getting their food and drinks. I didn't really notice it at the time, but now I realize he was thinking about what he was going to say. Once seated, we would all bow our heads and listen to his quiet and strong words. He would always think of the most perfect grace. It always included military and Foreign Service Officers' service to their country around the globe, and often reminded us to reflect on our country's leaders making difficult decisions.

In 1986, when I was in first grade, my mom was the leader of my Brownies Girl Scout troop and my father was national security advisor. He volunteered to bring me to work with him to sell cookies at the White House. I didn't have to work too hard. People at the White House were working long hours, as always, and my cookies were a hot commodity. To this day, I still have my cookie order form with some pretty famous names, with their preference for Thin Mints or Samoas duly noted.

CHAPTER SEVEN

SERVING *as* SECRETARY *of* DEFENSE

WHEN MY FATHER BECAME secretary of defense, my life didn't instantly change. At seven years old, the world I knew best and loved most was the wooded backyard of our home in McLean, Virginia. In the winter, when the trees were bare, you could see down the sloping hills to the Potomac River. In the spring, the new leaves sprouted electric green, and in the summer, I built many a hideout with my friends in the branches and leaves. This is the home my father came back to each night from the White House, or from his many trips overseas. This is the home where he and my mother spent some of their happiest times, and my father his last years. My mother still lives there, and it's an anchor in my life.

When we first moved into the house, I was delighted to find it had a "disco room" in the basement, complete with flashing multicolored lights, a dance floor, and a sound system. To my father's chagrin, the room was also located right next to his home office. I'd have friends over and we'd dance gleefully in the bright lights, doing our best Cyndi Lauper moves across the half-moon of the smooth dance floor. Once my friends and I had perfected our routine, I would wander into my dad's office and plead with him to watch our dance "performance."

Many things about the house have not changed, but the disco room did come down.

When looking back on photographs of the 1980s and 1990s, I see my father was always in one of three outfits: a suit, a bathing suit, or tennis whites. A few hundred feet from our front door was a tennis court co-owned by our neighbors, a lovely couple who often played doubles with my parents back then. Dad would happily play with anyone who had an interest, no matter how much of a talent or a novice they were. If a game time was set and it had rained the day prior, he would go up to our home court early to squeegee it or blow off the leaves, making sure it was ready for play. When he was traveling abroad, he always took his racquet with him. He was never one to cancel or miss a game.

So, in the mid-1980s you could often find me next to the tennis court, on the tennis court, or being instructed on how to properly hold a tennis racquet. As any child of parents who are fiercely dedicated to a hobby knows, you usually grow to love or hate whatever sport or pastime captivates your parents and demands so much of their time. I loved to play as a kid; as a teenager I began to dislike the competitive nature of the game, especially the intensity with which my parents played it. I turned my back on the sport permanently, or so I thought. After having kids of my own, I gradually began to play again, and now enjoy it several times a week.

Beside me courtside in the '80s you'd find our huge yellow Labrador, Salvador—named after my parents' friend in Portugal. I thought the name was ridiculous, even embarrassing. I didn't understand the connection to Portugal, and the name Salvador seemed downright silly to a six-year-old girl who thought "Spot" or "Scout" sounded far more suitable for a dog.

My father was the newly nominated secretary of defense, but he still had his two major jobs on the home front. One, he was responsible for taking out the trash. I don't mean walking the can down the driveway. Our driveway was long and winding and no large truck could navigate it, so we had to deliver our trash to the county. That meant that every Saturday morning my father would load up the trunk of his car with trash bags and drive down the road to meet the trash truck at the local elementary school. Because of this regular routine, he got to know the sanitation workers by name. As he got older and he could no longer navigate those Saturday morning trash runs, my mom would start to take the trash for him. The workers would always ask after him and send their best wishes.

His second job, and one that he also seemingly enjoyed, was cleaning the pool. My father was delighted to be able to afford a house with a pool. It required work, but he wasn't above doing that work himself. In fact, for some reason he relished skimming leaves off the surface, checking the chemical balance, and emptying the skimmers. And yes, he occasionally got in and swam too. When a knee injury slowed him down on land, swimming became his sport of choice.

I did know something dramatic and exciting was happening when my entire extended family trooped down to the White House on November 23, 1987. The video footage of President Reagan greeting all of us in the Oval Office is a sight to behold: lots of '80s hair, questionable fashion choices, and an especially awkward shot of me tucking my face into the folds of my mother's dress, mortified as she tells the president an embarrassing anecdote about me not understanding the nature of my father's new role.

And my father had to admit, "Being secretary of defense is very different than being deputy secretary. I was always in front of the public or the country."

When my father was confirmed as secretary of defense, it was his seventh confirmation hearing in nearly twenty years. He was by now a Washington insider and his reputation as "the consummate government bureaucrat" was solidifying. "He has served in seven agencies, from the Office of Economic Opportunity to the National Security Council to the Department of Health and Human Services, and done each job in a way that has enhanced his reputation for toughness, competence, and independence," *The New Republic* noted.[85] It only took a few weeks for him to be confirmed after nomination, which was quite quick. The final vote was ninety-one to one, which also shows that he had great bipartisan support.

The lone dissenter was Senator Jesse Helms—the same Republican from North Carolina who had opposed my father's confirmation as deputy secretary of defense. Helms considered Cap Weinberger as something of an arch-nemesis, and my father as Weinberger's acolyte. When Weinberger was being confirmed as secretary of defense and my father as deputy, Helms said Carlucci's "talents reinforce Mr. Weinberger's weaknesses and obviate his strengths."[86] When my father's own confirmation as secretary of defense came about, it was clear that Helms hadn't changed his point of view.

In his confirmation hearings, my father had to answer lots of questions about defense spending, which had increased dramatically over the course of the tenure of his predecessor.

Weinberger had resigned as secretary of defense on November 6, 1987, after six years and 306 days in the role. He was the third-longest-serving secretary of defense—only Robert McNamara and Donald Rumsfeld served longer in the role. Weinberger was known as a true Cold Warrior, whose mistrust of the Soviets never waned—this was one of the things that put him at odds with Secretary of State George Shultz. Shultz saw that once Gorbachev came to power, some measure of cooperation with the Soviets would be of great mutual benefit. As discussed in chapter 4, Weinberger and Shultz disagreed on plenty of other things as well and were in some ways each other's natural competitors. The *New York Times* noted,

> The sources of the conflict between the two men are partly institutional: The State Department's mission is to seek diplomatic accommodation, sometimes through the selective application of American military force abroad. The Defense Department, directly responsible for defending the nation's security against hostile powers, is often more conservative about improving relations with the Soviet Union and less willing to commit American forces to combat . . . But far more than is generally recognized, and to a far greater degree than in the past, the differences between Shultz and Weinberger reflect very different backgrounds and temperaments and a longstanding professional rivalry.

"There is a personal edge to the disputes between George and Cap that is much sharper than previous feuds," says a veteran national security official. "These guys have been rivals for fifteen years."[87]

As mentioned before, my father was one of the few men who got along with and understood both Weinberger and Shultz, and this made him very valuable to President Reagan. When my father became national security advisor in 1986, he recalled: "Ronald Reagan made his approach by saying, 'I'd like you to be my National Security Advisor because you're the only person that George Shultz and Cap Weinberger can agree on.' I wasn't sure if that was a very good qualification."[88]

Weinberger was well regarded in his role as secretary of defense and in the many other positions he held throughout his long career in government, but he was not a universally liked figure. As a brief Department of Defense biography of him summarized:

> International problems engaged much of Weinberger's time and attention, involving him in necessarily close relationships with other agencies that did not always go smoothly. Differences in policy on some issues between Defense and other organizations, especially State, sometimes led to friction and personality clashes. Weinberger did not get along well with the secretaries of state during his term—Alexander M. Haig (1981–82) and George Shultz (1982–89)—and he objected to the influence exercised by some National Security Council officials, including NSC advisor Robert McFarlane.[89]

When it came to the Iran-Contra affair, Shultz and Weinberger differed in their views again. Shultz was very outspoken in his disapproval of the scheme. Weinberger, though, helped facilitate the transfer of US missiles to Iran and then denied the depth of his knowledge and involvement. As it got harder for him to downplay his part in what happened, Weinberger signaled to Howard Baker, Reagan's chief of staff, that he was going to resign. After stepping down, Weinberger was indicted. In the end President George H. W. Bush pardoned him just before he and five other defendants were scheduled to go to trial in December of 1992.[90]

After everything that happened, and with Weinberger's preferred replacement, William Howard Taft IV, still under consideration, Howard Baker had to work to get my dad to consider the position. At first my father politely refused the role as secretary of defense, claiming he was happy where he was as national security advisor. Baker ultimately convinced him, promising my father that he would be quickly confirmed and that his successor as NSA, his deputy Colin Powell, was already well regarded and ready for the role. In a later conversation with President Reagan regarding Powell, my father indicated his firm confidence in Powell. "'Not only could he replace me, in my judgement Mr. President, but he'd be far better than I am in the job.' I said, 'I'm not seeking compliments. I just think he will be.' And as you know Colin did perform magnificently in the job."[91]

Colin Powell was ready to step in to replace my father as national security advisor, and he was totally acceptable to the president as national security advisor. Powell recounted to me how that went down:

> One morning we're having a staff meeting with the president . . . I was chairing the meeting by now. I had moved

into position, but below Frank and Shultz. And, so, we're having a meeting in the situation room . . . I was seen as the guy who sort of does all these things for Frank. I'm sitting at the head of the table. Shultz is there [but] Frank's not there and the president's not there. Well, let's keep going.

So, we go on for another fifteen minutes and I wonder where the hell are they? Suddenly the door opens, and the president walks in; he sits down at his head of the table. I'm at the other end. And Frank comes in and goes around to the side of the table and sits down. I don't know what's happened but they're here and the meeting continues. Frank rips off a piece of paper from a pad. I think I still have [the paper] somewhere. And he scribbled something on it and then he passes it down to a guy who passed it on to me. I'm paying attention to the meeting, but I finally open it up and it said, "Good luck, you're the national security advisor."

What? Nobody asked me. The president didn't interview me. Frank, you should have known better. You screwed me again. I'm stuck here again. But how do you say no to being the national security advisor? I never quite got over that. Frank just took it in stride—yeah, you're the new national security advisor. I don't know that we ever discussed it again. I'm the national security advisor of the United States of America, replacing Frank Carlucci who has just become the defense secretary.[92]

As mentioned previously, my father was named national security advisor due to his ability to be an effective go-between with Shultz and Weinberger. Describing his role as mediator, he said:

> I was constantly negotiating between those two. That started way back when I was with both of them in OMB. When I was deputy secretary of defense, I had proposed breakfast once a week between the two of them so they could try and see eye to eye . . . When I became national security advisor, I would have them once a week for lunch in the White House and we'd try and work out the differences, but they both had strongly held views. George put it best when I think he said, "Cap is a position taker and I'm more analytical." Cap is very quick to take positions—he's a lawyer—and George waits to take positions but both are equally tenacious once they've taken a position. It was just a question of chipping away and I tried to avoid having these issues come before the president but on occasion, I had to take the differences to the president to get them resolved.[93]

Will Taft spoke in a similarly humble fashion when I recently asked him about being passed over for the secretary of defense appointment. Taft had been serving as deputy secretary of defense and could well have expected to take on the secretary role when Weinberger stepped down. Instead, he became my father's deputy secretary of defense and briefly served as acting secretary when my father left at the end of the Reagan administration. As Taft graciously told me:

> Cap had wanted me to succeed him as secretary and Howard Baker, among others, thought that Frank would be a better secretary of defense. And I'm inclined to agree with him [Baker] on that. I know he was right. There still was some unhappiness, but Frank smoothed that over very well by

> assuring me that I would stay where I was, which was what I wanted to do . . . and I, as I say, I couldn't suggest that Frank wouldn't have been better than I was at that job. He was better than I would have been, at that time.[94]

As for my father's view on Taft, he said, "Will Taft is a very able individual . . . he tends to be underestimated by a lot of people, because of his personal style, which seems a little reticent. But he is not. He is capable of making decisions, and did a good job in the budget process . . . When I gave him the assignment of burden-sharing, he performed superbly."[95]

My father did not come into the position as secretary with an agenda per se. He admired Weinberger tremendously, but he did have a different perspective on some issues and his own personal management style. My father reflected, "I'm not known as a soft manager. On the other hand, I'm not a kick-'em-in-the-rear type who yells and screams and creates conflict. The way you manage is to create clear lines of authority and to set realizable and concrete goals."[96]

My father also handled relationships between departments differently than his predecessor.

> For example, [Secretary of State] George Shultz wanted to have direct contact with the chairman of the Joint Chiefs, Bill Crowe. Cap had objected to that. I had no objection to that. Cap had basically dragged his feet and found all kinds of reasons not to negotiate with his Soviet counterpart, Minister of Defense Yazov. I turned that around and negotiated with him. Cap had been pushing very hard for an early deployment of SDI. I had serious questions in my

> own mind as to the feasibility of early deployment, indeed the feasibility of the whole program. I commissioned a study which said, yes it will be feasible, but you've got to get the cost down. I worked harder at getting the cost down and moved SDI pretty much into the Pentagon system so that I could evaluate its priorities alongside other priorities, whereas Cap had kept it very much separate and above the kind of scrutiny some of the other programs went through. So there really were different things. That doesn't mean, by the way, that I didn't have very high regard for Cap. He was a great secretary of defense.[97]

My father did not dramatically deviate from the course that Weinberger set during his time as secretary, but he did put his own stamp on the job. As the *New York Times* later reported, "Though he was defense secretary for only fourteen months, Mr. Carlucci was not a caretaker. He presided over $33 billion in budget cuts, closing domestic bases while maintaining strength abroad as the Cold War wound down."[98]

As for the president he served under, my father said: "My view of Ronald Reagan was that he was conservative in his approach, no question, yet he was anything but a right-winger, and had a masterful touch in listening to people. He'd listen and then he'd leave the room and leave the problem to us. They all felt good that they'd had their day with the president. We were left with the problem, but that was our job."[99] My father had a regularly scheduled hour-long meeting with the president weekly, but he was given lots of leeway to make decisions independently.

From his own point of view, my father's most significant accomplishments as secretary were improving military negotiations with the Soviet Union, turning the defense budget around, working on infrastructure issues, and pursuing successful Middle East policies. On a day-to-day basis, he recalled:

> [A] vast majority of my time as secretary of defense was spent dealing with the Congress. I would call congressmen and senators daily to get our budget through, and to make sure our defense programs appropriations actually went for defense and not somebody's favorite domestic project. A substantial number of congressional calls were about getting a better airplane for congressional travel. After that, endless and repetitive testimony was given before committees.

Dealing with Congress and committees was not my father's favorite part of the job. Right as he took office, my father had to manage a major scandal within the Department of Defense. Once he was confirmed, he said he had one hour's notice that the attorney general was going to announce what was called "Illwind."[100] The biggest procurement scandal in the Pentagon's history, it was the result of a three-year investigation by the FBI into corruption by US government and military officials over defense spending. According to the FBI:

> [S]ome Defense Department employees had taken bribes from businesses in exchange for inside information on procurement bids that helped some of the nation's largest military contractors win lucrative weapons systems deals. More than sixty contractors, consultants, and government officials were ultimately prosecuted—including

> a high-ranking Pentagon assistant secretary and a deputy assistant secretary of the Navy. As a monetary measure of the significance of the crimes, the case resulted in a total of $622 million worth of fines, recoveries, restitutions, and forfeitures.[101]

The case led Congress to pass the Procurement Integrity Act in 1988, which was later amended in 1996. "Illwind" remains the largest and most successful investigation of defense procurement fraud in US history.[102] The investigation led to the freezing of all contracts and made an already difficult budget climate even more of a challenge.

The morale at the Pentagon was very low and my father was immediately faced with addressing the Department of Defense budget request for fiscal year 1989. The stock market crash in October 1987 didn't help matters. The administration and Congress had agreed that the 1989 Department of Defense budget would be around $299 billion, $33 billion less than President Reagan had requested. My father had to make some difficult decisions about how to deal with the shortfall. He chose to cut jobs in order to keep a proposed military pay increase and maintain training and support programs. He faced some pushback. The Navy objected to his order that it retire sixteen frigates—an issue important enough that Secretary of the Navy James H. Webb Jr. later resigned over it.

My father spent many hours working with Congress to approve the budget of the department and to garner support on the Hill, but even so, President Reagan vetoed the proposed defense budget in the summer of 1988. More negotiating ensued, and eventually an agreement was reached.

To help meet the leaner budget, my father began the first round of the Base Realignment and Closure (BRAC) commissions to close unnecessary and outdated bases. The BRAC commissions represent a compromise of power between the executive and legislative branches to facilitate the closing of military installments, usually for budgetary reasons, but also for broader strategic reasons. For example, BRAC commissions in the 1990s largely came in response to the dissolution of the Soviet Union and the reallocation of resources to conflicts in the Middle East. In short, the US Constitution does not outline how to manage military installations, and so for much of our country's history, this was largely the prerogative of the president. After large-scale closures of World War II–era infrastructure in the 1960s and 1970s, Congress enacted legislation in 1977 that limited the executive's ability to close or realign major military installations.[103]

Closing a military base or installation is a money-saving tactic. As my father pointed out in an interview, closing a base is usually the quickest way to cut major military costs. These funds can then be reallocated to ensure US soldiers have the latest and most effective tanks, aircraft, or other equipment. But it's a costly maneuver from a political standpoint. Military bases are the crux of the local economy, and many jobs are lost when one closes—most of them held by people not in uniform. Think of all the restaurants, salons, health-care facilities, shops, and other services offered by a local town to military personnel and their families who live on a large base.

Although they can cause considerable political backlash, it's clear that such closures are necessary for the continued evolution of our armed forces. Before going about this objective, my father reflected.

> Early on, I recognized that budget cuts were coming ("peace dividend") and that our infrastructure was far too large for our fighting forces. We were wasting a lot of money. But I had watched poor Elliott Richardson as secretary of defense get slaughtered by the Congress when he tried to close some bases. So, I looked for a novel way to do it. I spotted a bill that was introduced by Congressman Dick Armey that would set up a congressional base closing commission. I asked Armey to come see me and suggested to him we make it an Independent Base Closure Commission appointed by the secretary of defense. He bought that. I then tried it out on Les Aspin, the chairman of my House Committee, who said "Carlucci you're nuts." Tom Foley, then speaker of the house, said much the same thing. But Sam Nunn, chairman of my Senate committee, thought it was a good idea, as did his ranking minority member, John Warner.

When asked why he was so concerned about base realignments and closings, my father said:

> I felt that in good conscience I could not reduce the military establishment in size and capability without addressing this issue of scandalous waste. It was unfair to our military people. The idea was mine . . . I called in Aspin, Nunn, Dickenson, and Warner, and talked to them about a commission. They said, "Frank, you're not serious, do you really want to take on bases?"
>
> I said, "Yes, I want to take on bases."
>
> The president's reaction was much the same. He rolled his eyes and said, "Do you really want to do that?"[104]

It might not have been a popular position, but my father was clear that it was what was required at the moment, and he would see it done.

Aside from his duties on Capitol Hill, during his fourteen months as secretary of defense my father made thirteen trips abroad. An article produced by the Pentagon looking back at his career noted that this meant

> devoting about 25 percent of his time in office to visiting Europe, the Middle East, Africa, and Asia. The first incumbent secretary of defense to visit the Soviet Union, he went there twice . . . He visited NATO headquarters at Brussels four times during his term to discuss the future of NATO within the context of the shrinking US defense budget, arms control advances, and the changes taking place in the Soviet Union under Gorbachev's leadership.[105]

Admiral Bill Owens, my father's senior military assistant, was often in attendance with him on these trips. Owens went on to be the vice chairman of the Joint Chiefs of Staff under President Clinton, but he credited my father with truly launching his career, and he fondly recalled his many trips with my father when he shared some reminiscences with me:

> Frank came to the Pentagon and was well-known in diplomatic circles and in defense circles as well. He was soft-spoken and humble, and I was a young one-star admiral at the time. He was interviewing for a senior military assistant in the Department of Defense. Typically that's been a three-star job. There were many who have gone

through that job who then became more senior and more visible. Your dad had asked the Navy, apparently, for someone who would fit his personality. I don't really like talking about myself this way, but I'll just give you this explanation because it was unique and different given that I was young, and that no one would ever think that the secretary of defense would even want to talk to a one-star. Two or three others were interviewing and all of them were three-stars from the other services.

I loved your dad when I first met him. I almost get tears in my eyes when I think of the way he was. He was humble. He was very straightforward . . .

I was a nuclear submarine guy. We were typically put into a stove pipe that said these guys don't know much at all, except nuclear power and submarines. They don't know anything about aircraft carriers. They don't know about the Marines . . . [and it's true] I was not nearly as broad as other officers that he could have chosen. And so, I remember going down to see him and telling him, you know, that I was really honored to be chosen and to be by his side.

As it turned out, I would have done anything for Frank Carlucci. I was just totally loyal to him, this humble little man who had more experience than anybody I had ever known. It was just a great thing to be with him. And, as time went on it was great to be with your mom as well. I traveled with him almost all the time.

In those meetings, on those trips, Frank had a special way of introducing me to whatever head of state we were visiting or whoever it was; he didn't have to do that. I

> mean, I was, frankly, I was a peon there. I was there to serve him. He was a real gentleman about all of that.
>
> He had a broader perspective than any of the rest of us. He didn't show off about that, you could just see it from his responses and his preparation. He was always prepared. He was very smart. And so, for us, when we were trying to get him prepared, in fact, it frequently turned out to be that he would prepare us rather than the other way around. He usually knew many of the people in the foreign country we were going to visit, and I needed to get to know who they were. So, before we visited, he briefed me a little bit on who King Hussein [of Jordan] was, for instance. I remember later when I was the sixth fleet commander in the Mediterranean during the first Gulf War and then when I was the vice chairman [of the Joint Chiefs], I went to see Hussein and we could talk about Frank and how we met through Frank Carlucci.
>
> When we were together with King Hussein, it wasn't Frank and his hired hand; it was the three of us. It's an art form to be so humble that you're not afraid of having this young admiral say a few things in a meeting like that.[106]

The vast majority of these trips were colored by Cold War dynamics, and by the omnipresent threat of nuclear war. My father saw firsthand that President Reagan hated warfare, and in particular, nuclear weapons. Periodically, the president would say, "Let's get rid of the nukes." One day my father got a little exasperated. As he put it:

I guess I had gotten tired of making the argument that we need nuclear forces as a deterrent, so I said, "Mr. President, if you do that, Margaret Thatcher will be on the phone in five minutes."

"Oh no, I don't want that," he said.

Ronald Reagan adored Margaret Thatcher and vice versa. That seemed strange because they were different types of personalities. Margaret was a hard-driving, steel intellect who loved to focus on details and was extremely assertive. Ronald Reagan was much more laid back, loved jokes and couldn't wait to get through the cue cards. But they would come together on the issues once they had been negotiated by the respective staff. It was a uniquely productive relationship.

To state the obvious, negotiations with and about the Soviets were often tense. In 1987 the United States discovered that the Russians were building a radar station in Krasnoyarsk, Siberia, that would be in defiance of the 1972 Anti-Ballistic Missile Treaty. After balking and evading the allegations, they eventually admitted that the project was in fact in violation of the agreement and halted construction. When it was suggested that Weinberger visit the site, he refused to engage. My father tentatively agreed to meet Soviet Defense Minister Dmitry Yazov, but on neutral territory in Bern, Switzerland.

Weinberger refused to meet with Yazov in part due to an incident where the Soviet government refused to apologize for the accidental killing of Major Arthur D. Nicholson Jr. The event heightened tensions significantly between the United States and the Soviet Union. The *New York Times* reported that Nicholson was "a member of a two-man patrol on lawful assignment in territory that Soviet authorities claimed was off limits. He bled to death when Soviet soldiers prevented his partner from giving medical aid. Off limits or not, opening fire on him without warning was inexcusable."[107] Weinberger refused to meet with Soviet Foreign Affairs Minister Eduard Shevardnadze until the USSR issued an apology. My father wanted the apology too, but he also was willing to work with others to get it.

The first time my father met Dmitri Yazov was in Bern in March of 1988. The official reason for the trip was to open a "military dialogue" with Yazov, which would include a request for an apology for the Nicholson shooting in 1985. Bern, Switzerland, was chosen due to its neutral nature, as well as the fact it was close to the location of my great-great-grandmother's birthplace. In fact, before the historic meeting between the two defense officials, my father and mother went sightseeing in Schagnau, Switzerland, the birthplace of my father's maternal great-grandmother.

In recalling the meeting with the Soviet defense minister, my father wrote:

> Yazov was a big buff man who reminded me of a Soviet tank. I gave him a four-point agenda:
>
> Avoiding dangerous incidents;
> Discussing respective military doctrines;
> Military to military contacts;

> Arms control.
>
> I regarded the last as least important, although for the Soviets it was the most important. I set about learning Soviet military doctrine. At one point, I lectured two hundred of their top generals and admirals at the Voroshilov Military Academy on their doctrine, explaining why it was offensive in nature. One of them privately told me I had surprised them with my knowledge of their doctrine. On our second meeting I went to Moscow. As the meeting started, I asked, "Where is the apology for the brutal killing of Major Nicholson?" Yazov said they hadn't written it yet. I said, "Let's you and I meet privately." So, we went into Yazov's office with only the Soviet interpreter present. I effectively wrote the Soviet apology . . .

On June 16, 1988, an opinion piece in the *New York Times* noted that "during a discussion with Secretary Carlucci on May 31, Mr. Yazov said: 'I express my regret over the incident and I am sorry that this occurred. . . . I have agreed we will do all we can to prevent these kinds of incidents in the future.'"[108]

First mission accomplished.

My father helped to improve the communication between the US and Russian militaries significantly. The Soviet press ran pictures of my father visiting ships and airplanes that had very recently been Russian state secrets. The Soviet counterpart to Admiral Crowe, General Akhromeyev, paid a visit to the United States and told my father he was impressed by our military.

My father always kept Secretary of State George Shultz informed of his discussions. Shultz was largely supportive because he and my father were largely on the same page, but some of

Shultz's staff got a little bit nervous that the Defense Department appeared to be driving foreign policy. As my father wrote, "We played a significant role, but George was the conceptualizer."

According to my father, the Soviet military personnel who visited the United States came to appreciate how strong we were militarily and that our intentions were basically peaceful. This, coupled with George Shultz's creative way of looking at regional issues, began to soften the relationship between the United States and the Soviet Union.

The president, too, seemed satisfied with the way things were going. My father accompanied President Reagan when he made a famous visit to Moscow for the Moscow Summit in May 1988, where he discussed human rights and disarmament with Gorbachev. President Reagan was the first American president to visit the Soviet capital since President Nixon fourteen years prior. The growing rapport between the two leaders signaled the beginning of the end of the Cold War.

In August of 1988, my father traveled to Moscow again to visit Minister Yazov. My mother accompanied him. She recalled that it was an incredibly difficult trip; nobody spoke English, and she didn't speak Russian, so it was very challenging to come up with any kind of conversation with her counterpart, Emma Yazov.

After four days in Moscow, the US delegation was invited to Yalta. From there they took a barge to Sevastopol, home port of the Soviet Black Sea fleet, and Mr. Yazov proudly led his American guests on a tour of one of the newest warships in the Soviet Navy. It was likely the first time an American had ever boarded the ship, and the first time non-Soviets had entered Sevastopol in years.

Of course, my father being my father, he asked, "Where am I going to exercise?" The Soviets obviously didn't have a gym nearby. They came up with the idea that he could go out into the Black Sea and swim laps. So they cordoned off an area, set up some guards to keep watch, and surveilled my father swimming back and forth in the Black Sea.

Following the visit, my parents flew on to Ankara, Turkey. At the end of the trip everyone was exhausted and ready for a day of sunbathing and relaxing that had been planned in Izmir before heading back to the United States. At some point on the way to Turkey, my mother was told that the Turkish government was inquiring if "the minister would like to visit Ephesus." If so, they would be delighted to provide helicopters to transport the delegation.

My mother responded, "Yes, we would. Please thank the Turkish government. But please don't tell the minister." She knew my father well, that he was none too interested in visiting cultural sites, and that he would be sorely disappointed to learn his relaxation time was being compromised.

Later that evening my father found out about the plans to visit the ancient city of Ephesus. He was not pleased. My mother pleaded with him. "Yes, you are exhausted, but so is everyone else. And *think* about your heritage! Think about the opportunity to visit this historic site."

My father looked at her and said, "Rocks! We are going to see rocks!" But he went. And in the end, everyone had a great time.

The Cold War was waning, but it certainly wasn't over. My father still had a lot of work to do regarding disarmament and defense planning as tensions de-escalated. He noted,

> Gorbachev and Reagan were a study in contrast. Gorbachev couldn't wait to get to the schedule, made his own notes and talking points. Ronald Reagan would start by telling some jokes, was much more laid back, and went through the talking points quickly. There was not much back and forth other than Gorbachev going on and on about how SDI was so disruptive to our negotiations.

As defense secretary, my father commissioned a study about the feasibility of the SDI program and its huge costs. This moved SDI into the Pentagon system so he could keep tabs on it. Even if many doubted the SDI program, including most Americans, the important thing was that Gorbachev believed it and it gave Reagan leverage in negotiations. It was an important deterrent with the Soviets and also with other bad actors such as Libya.

As mentioned in chapter 6, that leverage SDI provided turned out to be invaluable. Following Reagan's visit to Moscow, the Intermediate-Range Nuclear Forces Treaty (INF Treaty) was enacted on June 1, 1988. The INF Treaty was a landmark arms control agreement between Reagan and Gorbachev, and the first time the two sides agreed to reduce their nuclear arsenals. It eliminated an entire category of nuclear weapons and employed extensive on-site inspections to ensure both sides were following the treaty. Approximately 2,692 short-, medium-, and intermediate-range missiles were destroyed by its implementation deadline of June 1, 1991. In 2019, under President Trump, the United States formally withdrew from the INF Treaty due to Russia's continued noncompliance.[109]

Overall, my father was a quiet but important navigator of Cold War policies and had more influence than many people realize. In a letter to President Reagan written in April of 1987 when my father was still national security advisor, he wrote:

> The wisdom of your four-part agenda for US–Soviet relations—arms reductions, easing regional conflicts, human rights, and bilateral contacts—is that it is not seasonal, but perennial; it is steady, but flexible; it can deal with positive as well as negative developments in Soviet behavior. The main purpose of your speech in Los Angeles will be to rearticulate this policy, to take stock of recent developments, and to remind Americans and Soviets of its underlying values and goals. It will contain some good news—promising Soviet moves on arms and human rights, along with big remaining problems; some bad news—continued Soviet failure to move positively on regional conflicts; clear statements on what it will take from the Soviets to move the relationship ahead; and a strong reminder to all that only the compass of freedom points to real peace and human progress.
>
> George Shultz must go to Moscow with his seatbelt securely fastened to your policy . . . George's foremost goals should be those he has fully under his control: Learning where the Soviets are coming from in this new tactical phase; and telling them clearly where we stand. This Moscow meeting is not the setting for negotiations, i.e., making changes on the spot in our positions, especially given the demeaning and insecure situation created by the Soviets at our embassy.

Reagan had ratcheted up the temperature of the Cold War by initiating the largest military buildup during peacetime, and he then worked to defuse tensions and dismantle some of what he had created. My father surmised that, despite their different styles, Gorbachev and Reagan hit it off because they both had the need to reach an agreement. In his memoirs, my father explained why he thought Reagan's strategy over the course of the Cold War was effective:

> Ronald Reagan broke the mold. He wanted to roll back communism. There's no doubt in my mind that negotiating from strength did the trick. Their military was impressed with our military, and they came to understand that our doctrine was defensive in nature. Moreover, it was hard for the Soviet people to understand why a US secretary of defense could be photographed roaming through a Blackjack bomber, when they had no access whatsoever to any military facilities.

The Blackjack was a sophisticated new aircraft that the Soviets had developed in secret, and my father was invited to see one on his second trip to the USSR, in August of 1988. As the *Chicago Tribune* explained,

> Carlucci and some of his aides were able to climb aboard the Soviet's top-secret Blackjack strategic bomber and later board a MiG-29 fighter jet. The Blackjack, which the Soviets claim is the largest and heaviest strategic bomber in the world, is roughly the equivalent of the US B-1 bomber and has a range of more than 4,500 miles without refueling.
>
> Ken Howard, the Pentagon spokesman, after watching the US team poke around the previously secret bomber

> said: "There are very few Air Force officers who have stood and looked into the (bomb) bay of a Blackjack. You are looking at all of them." The fact that a US secretary of defense was allowed such access was a remarkable event.[110]

The *New York Times* was more colorful in its coverage of the event.

> If a senior Soviet military officer had suggested two or three years ago that the American secretary of defense be invited to inspect the most advanced Russian warplanes, he probably would have been sent to a remote Siberian Army base if not a mental ward.
>
> The fact that Secretary of Defense Frank C. Carlucci spent one morning last week at Kubinka Air Base outside Moscow looking over the latest Soviet strategic bomber, known in the West as the Blackjack, was a reflection not only of changing relations between the superpowers but also of Mikhail S. Gorbachev's mastery over the military.
>
> In a subtle but significant shift in the balance of power, Mr. Gorbachev has reinforced the subordination of the military to the civilian Government and Communist Party leadership and regained the initiative from the defense establishment in setting military doctrine and defense policy.[111]

Though relations with the USSR dominated my father's tenure as secretary of defense, there were several other important issues and events he had to deal with. He recalled a few of these, one being the negotiation of the closure of a US base in Torrejón, Spain, where he had once been hospitalized with tuberculosis during his time in Portugal. Another was his negotiation of a base closure in the Philippines. Throughout his tenure, he also worked closely with NATO colleagues to keep the NATO alliance strong. "In my judgment, they were not doing enough. We were carrying most of the burden," he noted in his memoirs.

Another of the most important incidents of his time as secretary of defense involved not the USSR but Iran. As national security advisor, my father had been involved in the Kuwaiti Reflagging Operation, dubbed Operation Earnest Will, which essentially involved reflagging Kuwaiti ships with American flags so we could provide escorts to protect them from Iranian aggression. This was the United States Navy's largest and most complicated operation since World War II.[112] The Iranians were becoming more and more aggressive, harassing ships and even sending a flotilla to threaten Saudi Arabia as a part of the larger Iran-Iraq War that lasted from 1980 to 1988. Kuwait, one of Iraq's main allies at the time, was targeted by Iran as it attempted to exert naval control over the Persian Gulf. Iran was using small boats to place mines in the Gulf under the cover of night.

By the time my father came over to the Pentagon, tensions in the Gulf were high. My father and Admiral Crowe then conducted an operation that led to the sinking of about half the Iranian Navy in about twenty-four hours: on April 18, 1988, Operation Praying Mantis was launched in retaliation for the inadvertent mining of the USS *Samuel B. Roberts*. The operation led to the destruction of two Iranian surveillance platforms and the sinking of two ships, with another severely damaged.[113]

A month later, the USS *Vincennes,* which was in the region to protect the *Samuel B. Roberts* as it was escorted back to the United States for repairs, shot down Iran Air Flight 655, killing all 290 aboard. The *Vincennes* mistook the Iranian Airbus for an attacking fighter.

As my father wrote of the incident,

> I had one experience that was very disturbing. One night, I got a call about 2 a.m. from the chairman of the Joint Chiefs, Admiral Crowe, reporting that one of our ships might have shot down an Iranian F14. I hung up and started to go back to sleep when another call came. It was Admiral Crowe again. It was not an F14. It was an Airbus. I instantly went to the Pentagon and discovered the Airbus had not been squawking the proper code and was on a descending path heading towards the USS *Vincennes*, a guided missile cruiser. At the same time, the cruiser was surrounded by small boats firing at it. Admiral Crowe and I went down to a mock-up where we assumed the roles of captain and navigator. We concluded that the captain had made an honest mistake in shooting down the aircraft, but that was a very tragic event.
>
> At one point, the Iranians came out into the Gulf and fired a missile at our ships. Under the rules of engagement, our ships could defend themselves. I went to the president, through Colin, and said I wanted authority to react strongly. Back came the word "go to it" and we sank one of their ships, the Alvand. They had only two frigates. One of our planes was circling over the second frigate ready to

drop a laser-guided bomb onto a smokestack when Admiral Crowe said to me, "I think we've shed enough blood."

I said, "All right, call it off." He brought the plane back, but I suspect now that frigate is back out today causing trouble, and that I may have made a mistake in not sinking it.

We maintained a strong presence in the Gulf. We escorted ships and allowed them to reflag so we were defending the American flag. The Saudis provided facilities for us, but they were not doing enough in my judgment. I met with the King, who gave me a lecture on how important Saudi Arabia was to the United States. He got up to dismiss me and I said, "Oh custodian of the 'Two Holy Mosques,' if Saudi Arabia is important to us, it's also important to you and you need to participate in the defense of your country. Our seamen are out there in hot engine rooms patrolling the Gulf, making sacrifices while your ships are comfortably tied up alongside the pier. If you don't get your ships out there, I'm going to pull our ships out." I went back to Washington and George Shultz backed me up on this. So, the Saudis became more active.

Conflicts around the globe consumed my father's attention in the waning days of his tenure as secretary of defense. In particular, he was convinced that rebuilding our military before we negotiated with the Russians was the key factor to our winning the Cold War.

Credit is also due to George Shultz who mapped out the game plan for the president. And, of course, there is credit for the president himself who never wavered on the

> essential points. It's true Ronald Reagan did not involve himself in detail. It's also true that he trusted some people that did not merit that trust. Nor did he have a detailed knowledge of world affairs. But he had an optimistic demeanor, an unbounded faith in a free country, great instincts and a willingness to stand up and be counted. It was my privilege to have worked for him. I also enjoyed knowing Nancy, who was always considerate to me and was clearly very devoted to "Ronnie."
>
> Serving in the Reagan administration was a distinct honor. The jobs weren't easy and criticism flowed freely, but I learned to take it. There's no doubt in my mind that Ronald Reagan's approach in rebuilding America's strength before negotiating contributed to the success of negotiations and to the collapse of the Communist empire. All of us who knew Ronald Reagan liked him and tried to give him our full support. We particularly admired his optimistic vision of the United States and his flexibility in being willing to negotiate with a country he once termed "the evil empire."

My father always cited the people surrounding him as indispensable to his success as secretary of defense. He often gave credit to his superb military assistants, including Air Force General Gordon Fornell and Admiral Bill Owens. Chairman of the Joint Chiefs of Staff Bill Crowe became a close friend and confidant. My father remembered Crowe as

> a wonderful man; great sense of humor, very easy to work with, commands a lot of respect from the services. He didn't have the public flair of Colin Powell, but he was a

very solid, serious man who did not hesitate to step up to the difficult jobs. I can remember when the USS *Vincennes* shot down the Iranian Airbus . . . One of the things you obviously have to do is go out and tell the press. Bill Crowe immediately volunteered to do that. We all know that initial reports are never accurate, and the press takes them as accurate no matter how many times you say they are not going to be accurate. We always get castigated if those reports differ from subsequent reports. That, of course, happened in this case. I probably should have done the press conferences. I cite that as an example of Bill Crowe's willingness to step forward and take the heat. Crowe's role in the dismemberment of the Soviet Union was [also] pivotal and it's really never been told.

My father left office on January 20, 1989, when the George H. W. Bush administration came into power. There was some speculation that he might be asked to stay on. As *The New Republic* magazine wrote at the time:

> Before the race for the Republican presidential nomination was decided, *Business Week* said "there's talk in Republican circles" that either George Bush or Bob Dole "might want to keep Carlucci around to finish the job he started." Last month *TIME* upped the ante, calling Carlucci the only rising star in the twilight of the Reagan administration, and suggesting not only that he would be a "natural holdover" in a Bush administration at Defense or State, but that (according to "speculation") he "might continue to head the Pentagon in a Dukakis administration."[114]

In the end, George H. W. Bush won the election and named Dick Cheney as his secretary of defense. William Taft would serve as the acting secretary for the sixty days in between their appointments. There were some rumblings that Bush and Reagan had a somewhat frosty relationship, and Bush wanted to clean house. Bush did release his predecessor's entire cabinet, apart from Jim Baker, then secretary of the treasury, who had been Bush's campaign chairman. I didn't hear it from my father directly, but I've learned in recent times that my father was somewhat disappointed not to be asked to continue on in some capacity with the Bush administration. Over the ensuing years he was approached for a number of other potential appointments but respectfully declined. Reflecting on his time as secretary of defense and the security challenges of the future,

> Carlucci said he was most proud of three accomplishments: persuading Congress to agree to streamline base closing procedures, the conduct of the successful tanker escort operation in the Persian Gulf, and the development of a new, positive relationship with Soviet military authorities. Other achievements included setting funding priorities and guiding the process for cutting the FY 1989 Pentagon budget; developing a calm, measured approach to the Pentagon procurement fraud investigation; impressing on world leaders the dangers of long-range missile proliferation; and persuading Congress to drop the idea of using military forces to seal US borders in the fight against drugs. Carlucci said his biggest disappointment was that the Pentagon had "not been able to preserve the defense consensus" in Congress and in the nation at a

time when developments in the communist world showed that "negotiating from strength works." In an article published soon after his retirement, he listed what he considered the central challenges policymakers would face in the 1990s: the emergence of new and dangerous threats to US security from all over the world, the persistence of the Soviet threat, and the probability that the Western countries would face a growing tendency toward conflict arising from economic competition.[115]

My father hadn't accomplished everything he had hoped while in office, but as *TIME* magazine noted, "As a fresh and energetic figure in an administration rapidly drawing to its close, he has brightened his already lustrous reputation—and just possibly his future as well."[116]

His future was bright indeed, in a way that he had no means of anticipating. Against the odds, he was finally about to become the businessman his father had always wanted him to be.

CHAPTER EIGHT

BECOMING *a* BUSINESSMAN

BY 1989, MY FATHER had spent close to his entire career in public service. The accounts, both his and mine, shared so far in this book have hopefully shown you the kind of person he was and how he rose through the ranks as an official. I hope they have also given you insights into his different roles and responsibilities. He reached the pinnacle of government, worked under seven presidents—four directly and three during his years in the military and Foreign Service—served as national security advisor and secretary of defense. Then, when he could have just relaxed or settled into a comfortable retirement, he did the opposite. He tackled an entirely new career as a businessman and became just as successful, if not more successful, in this line of work than he had ever been before.

I was nine when my father left government, and had no real concept of what was happening or how life was changing. For me, it felt like his departure barely registered. But the year after my father left office, I did have a formative experience when I was able to visit the Soviet Union and China with my parents. I had never been invited to travel with my parents when my father was in office, but as soon as he left, he took the opportunity to bring me along. As a member of the board of directors of a company with interests abroad, he was invited to visit the USSR and China in 1990. The trip allowed him to reengage connections he had made years prior, and to forge new opportunities for bilateral collaboration as the Cold War was rapidly ending. The Berlin Wall had fallen in November of 1989, and the Baltic States and the Caucuses were quickly demanding independence from Soviet control.

In May of 1990, my mother pulled me out of fifth grade and handed me a *Simpsons* notebook with a picture of Bart Simpson on the front writing "No Class Today" on a school chalkboard. She instructed me to keep a journal of our trip—and so I did.

I didn't spend much time with my father on that trip to Moscow. Instead, my mother and I spent much of our time with Russian Defense Minister Dmitry Yazov's wife, Emma, and Yazov's granddaughter, Kate. Kate was about my age, with short blonde hair cut to frame her face, and no doubt was trotted out to be helpful and comforting to me. I don't remember her speaking any English. A photo taken in front of the Kremlin features me, my mom, Kate, Emma Yazov, and one additional woman who I assume was Yazov's daughter, as well as two members of the Soviet military. No other visitors are visible. No one is smiling. Nobody looks particularly comfortable.

At a large formal dinner in a wood-paneled private dining room, Yazov presented me with a large brown stuffed bear. I was awkward and silent, but politely accepted the gift. It was almost my size. My mom whispered in my ear, "Tell him you are going to name it *Vodka*." Much like my thoughts on the name of our beloved dog Salvador, I had no idea what vodka was or why I was naming my new stuffed animal this strange name. But I did as I was told. I told Yazov that I was giving my new Soviet bear this strange Soviet name. My mother was right: Yazov was thrilled and amused beyond measure that the little American girl had come up with such a clever name for her gift.

The economy of the USSR was in ruins at the time. Since I was a child, I didn't know this, but I saw the consequences of it, and I noted that the subway rides cost less than a penny. My mother and I went shopping at an outdoor market for gifts to bring home. We found a small painting of St. Basil's Cathedral that we wanted to buy. I don't know what exactly the exchange was between my mother and the vendor, but I remember feeling petrified, as my mother firmly instructed me to "wait here" as she accompanied the vendor to a nearby alley to complete the purchase. My heart was racing. She was paying him in dollars instead of rubles, an act that was illegal in the USSR but very desirable for both my mother and the vendor. I still have that small framed painting hanging in my home today. In my journal I noted other traditionally Russian things we did. We ate hardboiled eggs and brown bread for breakfast, we saw the Moscow ballet, we went to a military art gallery, and we went to a Soviet circus.

In November of 1990, my parents and I left Moscow for the People's Republic of China. That country, too, was in the midst of great political turmoil, but as a ten-year-old, I wasn't aware of it.

The Tiananmen Square Massacre had happened only a year before, and most US citizens had evacuated the country. US–China relations were tense, but officially, the US still maintained diplomatic ties with China. I don't know the official reason for our visit, but I can guess it was another effort on the part of the Chinese to maintain soft channels of diplomacy with the United States.

We were taken on a guided visit of China's major tourist attractions: the Forbidden City, Tiananmen Square, the Great Wall, the Ming Tombs. In the photos, there are no tourists. In my mind and in my journal, I noted the cold weather, the massive numbers of bicycles and lack of cars on the streets. Photos show me for the awkward preteen I was, posing in my oversized colorful jackets, sweaters, and jeans that look strange amid the monotone background of Communist China in the winter. My father is dressed in a khaki trench coat befitting a former US government official; my mother wore a 1980s suit, with shoulder pads and colored tights.

Again, we partook in long dinners, strange food, and diplomatic engagements. At one long dinner I excused myself to go to the bathroom and ended up wandering back through the hallways, finding a comfortable red bench, and falling asleep. Unfortunately for me, a few minutes later my absence was noted, and I was awakened and pulled back into the dining room for what seemed like a forever-long dinner for a young girl.

We went shopping for souvenirs and came home with dolls and a large wooden pagoda for my bedroom. My father spoke to students in a high school in Suzhou, we visited a silk embroidery research institute in Nanjing, and we attended a fashion show. When we got home from our travels, it was time for my father to reinvent himself and his career once again.

As he recalled, "When I left the Department of Defense, I was asked by four younger men to join them in their new merchant bank, that is to say a private equity house. They had already started it, but they needed somebody to put them on the map and to help them raise money." To say those four men were successful in this new enterprise would be a massive understatement. Each of them is now incredibly wealthy, to a degree they could not have imagined when their idea was hatched. They named the merchant bank The Carlyle Group, an homage to the Carlyle Hotel in New York, where two of the founders came up with the idea for the firm; they thought it sounded dignified, and benign enough to build a business around. My father wrote that he "found the concept attractive. They wanted to give me twenty percent of the group . . . I said no to that. I wanted to serve on outside boards so I would take a lower percent (I think about ten percent)."

While writing this book, I spoke with David Rubenstein, one of the cofounders of Carlyle Group, and he recounted for me his version of events of these early days of the private equity firm that has now become one of the most profitable in the world. According to Rubenstein, the original founders had asked my father for a meeting when he was still secretary of defense, and they were just starting out. Carlyle had gotten a great lease on an impressive building in DC, so they looked legitimate despite still being very much in startup mode. My father pulled up to the meeting in a government limo. Rubenstein and my father had a cordial meeting. My father knew he was interested in joining a host of corporate boards when he left office but also wanted a "perch," where he could hold a named position and be involved with a single company or firm. Rubenstein liked that my father was well respected and well connected and could introduce

Carlyle to potential contacts in the defense industry in the United States and around the world. It turned out that both Rubenstein and my father had been involved in the Carter administration—a significant point of connection. So, they struck a deal, and my father became vice chairman of Carlyle in 1989. He later went on to become chairman in 1993, a position he held until 2003.

It's noteworthy to pause here and reflect that those who reach the upper echelons of government service will often transition into a government-adjacent position with a lobbying firm or a consulting firm and take on "Beltway bandit"–type jobs. Most of these ex-officials are not more than a step or so removed from their former careers and circles. My father took a bigger leap into true private enterprise, and he helped to lay the groundwork for one of the most successful private equity buyout firms in the world.

As for those outside boards he spoke of, my father did join many of them—so many that it became the subject of some controversy, which I'll discuss in a moment. But as with anything that he did, my father did not sign up for something if he couldn't deliver at the highest level. He served on private sector boards including the boards of telecommunication companies, distribution companies, and, *yes,* some defense companies. He also sat on the boards of several NGOs, nonprofits, and educational institutions. The breadth of his expertise and depth of involvement in such a diverse group of entities highlights a truly unique private sector contribution that was by no means a footnote to his government career.

My father was going all but nonstop in these years, but in 1994 a serious health scare did force a brief pause. For a man who was so incredibly healthy, it seems absurd that at the age of sixty-four he would have emergency quintuple bypass surgery, but that's exactly what happened. I was a freshman in high school, but I only remember bits and pieces of this episode because, frankly, that's what he wanted. I believe he didn't want me to know how serious his condition was. I wasn't told about his surgery until a family member picked me up from school and brought me to the hospital as he was being whisked into the operating room. I remember standing in the hallway as they rolled the gurney through the swinging doors. He let go of my hand saying, "I'll be fine. *Go back to school.*" I did as he told me.

And even then, I didn't understand how serious it was. I remember talking to a friend during his recovery and she asked me, "Are there even five arteries in the heart to bypass? Isn't that *all* of them?"

My father made a full recovery, but he couldn't ignore the fact that he was mortal. Over the ensuing years he had three rotator cuff surgeries (likely as a result of hitting too many tennis balls during his lifetime). The biggest and final health challenge was to come when he was diagnosed with Parkinson's disease in 2004. But after his heart surgery in 1994, he still had plenty of good years, lucrative years, ahead.

Later he recalled, "I helped move [Carlyle] overseas. I identified the first major acquisition, BDM, [a defense contractor] which made them a credible player. We then went on to acquire a series of defense companies. Carlyle grew very fast, and defense is now only a minor portion of their activities."

My father was far from the only high-ranking official to join Carlyle. Others who joined after leaving office included former Secretary of State Jim Baker, President George H. W. Bush, and British Prime Minister John Major. But my father was the first of the Washington insiders to join, helping to set the mold and create the business model that would make Carlyle so successful in its early days. By 2001 the group was purported to be the largest private equity firm in the world.[117]

When I spoke to David Rubenstein, he told me that my father's likability and attitude were a big part of why he was invited into the firm. "Frank was always accessible. And he knew everybody in Washington, [at a time when] we didn't know everybody. And he was obviously a very likable person . . . He was willing to call people and he was great at opening doors. If we asked him to pick up the phone and call someone, he would. He gave us great credibility doing defense and aerospace deals."[118]

Not all of the Washington types Carlyle brought in worked in lockstep with each other—oversized egos sometimes tripped people up. I learned that when Carlyle courted Jim Baker to join the firm after he left office as secretary of state, Baker was a bit touchy about being seen as a subordinate to my father, the once secretary of defense, now chairman of Carlyle. Apparently Baker refused to join until given the adjacent-sounding position of "senior counselor," rather than any title that could be construed as reporting to my father as his boss.

As mentioned above in the excerpt from my father's memoirs, one of the first deals my father helped Carlyle complete was the purchase of BDM, a defense consulting firm. It marked the beginning of an era, and a profitable pattern: "BDM was one of Carlyle's first and most successful leveraged buyouts, part of a $1.8 billion run of profits Carlyle amassed for investors from 1992 to 2002 in the defense sector."[119]

The group was not without its critics. In a scathing cover story entitled "The Access Capitalists," written for *The New Republic* in 1993, the now best-selling author Michael Lewis said:

> Six years [after its founding] The Carlyle Group—the name was inspired by the New York hotel and chosen because, like "merchant bank," it sounded old and established—holds a majority stake in a dozen or so companies, which employ about 45,000 people and generate about $5 billion in revenues annually, principally from the United States government.
>
> Former Treasury Secretary Donald Regan, former Bush Campaign Chairman Fred Malek, former first son George Bush Jr., former CIA director Robert Gates and current SEC Chairman Arthur Levitt are advisors to, investors in, or board members of Carlyle's companies. . .

The author added,

> Carlyle's chief innovation was to insert the former defense secretary systematically into leveraged buyouts. Carlucci was ideally suited to the task. He still had a bit o' the old glitz. He possessed a reservoir of goodwill with the defense contractors who were the main sellers of businesses. (The result, no doubt, of his having spent billions of taxpayer dollars on items for our national defense.) And his presence conferred a self-fulfilling financial credibility on a deal.
>
> Over the next four years The Carlyle Group was able to exploit Frank Carlucci's connections within the industry, and within the Pentagon, to turn itself into one of the twenty-five largest defense contractors in the world . . . [120]

Although my father and The Carlyle Group had no doubts about the legitimacy of the company and the way it conducted business, after 9/11 Carlyle nevertheless felt it needed to distance itself from defense industry contracts. My father, Baker, and a host of others agreed to retire. They had done nothing wrong, but Carlyle wanted to address the unsubstantiated rumors circling the firm at the time about its connections in the Middle East, and this was a public way to do it.

My father remembered, "[Carlyle] shifted gears when I left; they brought in Lou Gerstner, former CEO of IBM, to take my place and began to grow even more rapidly. Today The Carlyle Group is arguably the world's largest private equity house with vast holdings, over $200B in assets under management. Needless to say, Carlyle solved my financial problems . . . "

My father had helped expand The Carlyle Group's investments into areas other than defense, including global telecommunications, a direction they further pursued after bringing in Gerstner after my father's departure—an obvious choice given his time as head of IBM. As I mentioned, Carlyle was also intentionally trying to transform its image. *The Washington Post* noted, "Carlyle officials resent being viewed as a stud farm for statesmen, siring fortunes merely through political connections. 'We would like to get away from the distractions of people sort of using that as an old chestnut that keeps on coming up,' one Carlyle source said, acknowledging that Gerstner's presence ought to help reshape public perception."[121]

In a lengthy profile on Rubenstein a year later, the *Post* went a little further:

> [Carlyle] has developed a reputation as the CIA of the business world—omnipresent, powerful, a little sinister. Media outlets from the *Village Voice* to *BusinessWeek* have depicted Carlyle as manipulating the levers of government

> from shadowy back rooms . . . Rubenstein resents the suggestion that Carlyle's bigwigs shape public policy for private gain . . . Still, he knows why people believe that about Carlyle. He even takes the blame for it. "I probably failed in conveying the idea that we're not using this company in an inappropriate way," he says.
>
> Now, bit by bit, Rubenstein wants to change that image. A year ago he hired his first public relations specialist. Then, in November, he replaced former Defense Secretary Frank Carlucci as Carlyle's chairman with a different type of heavyweight: Louis V. Gerstner Jr., the former chairman of IBM.[122]

My father maintained a chairman emeritus role for a number of years after he retired from being chairman. On the occasion of his death, The Carlyle Group remembered him with the statement: "Frank was instrumental in transforming our boutique investment firm into a respected global institution. His wisdom, knowledge, and stature helped us make smarter [investment] decisions and form fruitful relationships around the world."[123]

Rubenstein put it more bluntly: "I would say, you know, it was a good deal for both of us. He gave us credibility in the beginning; and in the end, I think he made a fair amount of money."

Incidentally, the firm continued to grow and diversify. In 2020 and 2021, The Carlyle Group ranked as the fourth-largest private equity firm in the world.[124] It has twenty-seven offices across five continents and manages $276 billion in assets.[125]

While my father's "perch" at Carlyle turned into far more than merely a place to hang his hat, he did also join many corporate and nonprofit boards after leaving office, just as he made known he intended to do. Perhaps he felt he was making up for lost time, now that he was making money in a way he could never have while in government.

The corporate boards of which he was a member included those of General Dynamics, Westinghouse, Upjohn and Northern Telecom, Ashland Oil Inc., Bell Atlantic Corp., Kaman Corp., Quaker Oats, and Connecticut Mutual Life Insurance. As for non-profits and other types of organizations, the groups that meant the most to him were the Center for Excellence in Education, the American Academy of Diplomacy, and most of all, the nonpartisan think tank RAND—which also became very important to me personally, for reasons I'll explain.

In the early to mid-1990s questions occasionally arose concerning how effective my father could be in managing so many responsibilities at once, but he answered these criticisms not with retorts or protestations, but by showing up and performing his duties. Even in a *Washington Post* article in 1993, written with the express purpose of criticizing all of his board positions, the journalist Kathleen Day reluctantly noted, "Spokesmen for companies on whose boards Carlucci serves seem unanimous in their praise for his contribution, citing his intelligence, experience, and, in the words of a Northern Telecom spokesman, 'stellar' attendance record."[126]

Michael Rich, former president of RAND, recounted to me recently that my father didn't do anything half-heartedly. If he was on the board, he would do the work. He would attend the board meetings in person. He flew to each and every one and participated in full each time. When asked by a reporter how he did it, my father said, "With hard work and long hours. It's not an impossible task. It requires a rigorous schedule; it requires physical stamina."[127] Despite slowing down physically somewhat following his heart surgery, my father was as dedicated as ever to the work he was doing.

His allegiances to some of these companies and groups ran deep and would not have been obvious to the casual onlooker or insult-hurler. One example is Connecticut Mutual Life Insurance. My father joined the company board in no small part because it was where his father had worked so many years ago, and he likely felt an allegiance to the company for that reason. I imagine he was honoring his father in some way, even if he didn't spell that out explicitly to anyone.

The expertise he offered was more than mere "access capital." I'm not denying that's an element of why organizations want well-known individuals on their boards. And clearly that was a part of my father being asked to join Carlyle. To be candid, on every board there is the hope, if not the expectation, that a board member will help "connect the dots" for companies. But my father cared deeply about the work he was doing, and he invested himself completely in it. He always kept current on domestic and world events; he was a total news junkie. He had a day-to-day awareness of the large-scale and global factors that were driving big trends.

From the 1990s through the mid-2000s, the world underwent a phase of rapid globalization. My father's understanding of geopolitical affairs along with his connections from his years in government service put him in a great position to be a known and trusted advisor to these boards as they opened international offices, invested, and bought companies overseas. The world was beginning to operate more globally than locally, so a man who had spent forty years working with a multidimensional understanding of the world was a valuable commodity. Most American businessmen don't have that skill set today—and they certainly didn't in the 1990s. He was a valuable advisor, and that's what an advisor should be—someone who can provide sound and credible advice and counsel to executive management.

Not only did he provide advice and counsel to companies and nonprofits during that time, but he also provided advice and counsel to friends, family, and former colleagues. My brother sought his counsel when he started his own IT business, and when I asked him to come speak to my master's class in strategic studies at Johns Hopkins, he willingly obliged. He took his duties to pass on his knowledge seriously. Despite his natural inclination to avoid the press and the limelight, Dad sat on countless national security and former secretary of defense panels. During these years his time became his most precious commodity, and he gave of it willingly and without reserve. He was both trying to make money for his family in his career as a businessperson, and he was trying to give back the knowledge he had gained from being a government servant.

One of the positions my father most enjoyed and spent the most time on was serving on the board of trustees for the RAND Corporation. In fact, it was the only board my father sat on west of the Mississippi. He disliked traveling long distances at this point, and he was also committed to being in-person for meetings whenever possible, so he confined most of his activities to the East Coast. For RAND he made an exception.

The RAND Corporation was founded in 1948. It had originated as a research and development (hence the name) program of the California-based Douglas Aircraft Company, a key supplier of World War II planes and aerospace weapons. In the aftermath of the war, RAND became an independent entity with the lofty mission: "To further and promote scientific, educational, and charitable purposes, all for the public welfare and security of the United States of America."[128] In essence, the bipartisan organization focused on military and defense, systems analysis, and public policy. Today it's still one of the most trusted sources of evidenced-based research in the United States, with expertise in issues that range from gun control to health care.

My father first joined RAND's board of trustees in 1983 but stepped down while serving as national security advisor and again when he became secretary of defense. While secretary of defense, he communicated frequently with experts at RAND who were doing research on national security topics. When I interviewed former RAND President Michael Rich (who joined the organization as a summer intern in 1975), he recounted the following interaction, the text of which I've edited slightly for clarity:

> As the Cold War was coming to an end, the handwriting was on the wall . . . the defense budget was going to decline. The military services began looking for new missions to slow the reductions, and they seized on the idea of expanding the use of military forces for drug interdiction. The idea was gaining momentum when President Reagan nominated your father to become secretary of defense in 1987. But we had just completed an analysis, called *Sealing the Borders*,[129] that concluded that the military should not expand its role in drug interdiction because of the way that illicit drugs, especially cocaine, were smuggled into the United States. Most of the trafficking was happening in very small boats that were essentially disposable to the smugglers: a boat could be captured and the crew detained, but the smugglers had a plentiful supply of more

> boats. It just wasn't a cost effective use of military forces. I sent the manuscript to your father and he took it along on one of his trips to the Middle East in the aftermath of an operation called Nimble Archer, in which the US Navy attacked two Iranian oil platforms. He read the analysis on the flight and when he got back to Washington, he put an end to the quest for an expanded military role in drug interdiction. As you know from your own years at RAND, our mission is to have a positive effect on policy with our analysis, it's not just to publish reports. This time it felt like the effect happened overnight.[130]

Obviously the RAND folks had deservedly earned a lot of credibility with my father.

After he left office as the secretary of defense, my father rejoined the RAND board in 1989 and served almost without break until 2007, when he became a trustee emeritus.

❋❋❋

During these years my father wasn't at home much, but he made the most of his time with me and my mother. I became a horse-obsessed teenager and my mother spent much of her time ferrying me around to barns all over Northern Virginia. My father had no real interest in horses, or animals of any kid, but he was pleased I was happy. In high school, I would often ask him for help with my schoolwork—especially foreign languages. I remember trotting downstairs to his den. He would be sitting in his chair, watching the news, and I'd ask him how to say something in French. He would say it quickly, as I would frantically try to write it down. I'd ask him how to spell it, and he would laugh. He told me he never learned how to write or spell in any of the half dozen languages he learned. He learned to speak them by talking to people, by working in the country. It seemed like a sixth sense; I was consistently amazed by how easily languages seemed to come to him.

He also served as my driving instructor when I got my learner's permit. The year was 1995 and I was eager to hit the road. My mom, perhaps rightly, was a nervous wreck when forced to ride in the passenger seat. She always had her hands glued to the passenger-side door—as if she would have to make an emergency exit at any moment—and she stomped her feet energetically, as if trying to push an invisible brake pedal on the floor. For my part, I wasn't terribly enthusiastic about her "helpful" commentary about my driving. Dad, on the other hand, was a teenager's delight. He would climb into the passenger seat, pull out a newspaper, and sit silently and happily while I drove him around. This was a good analogy to his parenting strategy, I think. He trusted me to be a good kid. I knew what was expected of me—good grades and good behavior. I didn't want to disappoint him, and that was enough.

Dad was home on the weekends, and at night for celebrations and important events. When he was home, he partook in daily tennis matches and always, too, in family dinners. On the weekends he liked the daily ritual of household chores like the aforementioned cleaning of the pool, and he would often mow our small lawn (if I had neglected to do it earlier). Given how much of his life he had spent and was still spending in meetings, he wasn't much for organized social activities; he preferred to stay home. My mom, on the other hand, loved to go to dinner parties, soirees, and cocktail parties in Washington, DC. She was skillful at convincing my father to go to these events, with the promise that they could leave after the dinner and before the dancing started. The détente would last for hours: my father might have been a key figure in helping to defuse the Cold War, but my mom was no slouch when it came to negotiating. However, once out the door and at an event, my father did remember that he liked to dance. Despite earlier protestations, he could often be found at least once or twice on the dance floor over the course of the evening.

I went off to college and graduated from Duke University with a degree in public policy in 2002. I had heard my father talk glowingly about RAND over the years, and I was thrilled to receive a job offer there as a research assistant, a position that matched my interests in international affairs and policy.

I headed out west to Los Angeles with little more than a few pieces of luggage and a lot of excitement for a new adventure living on the West Coast. As it turned out, soon after I arrived, I met my future husband, Josh. We worked on the same floor of the original two-story RAND building in Santa Monica. We met in the old copy room, where I came to his aid in a fight with an obstreperous fax machine. I learned he was at the Pardee RAND Graduate School getting his PhD; he'd been selected to do so through a special program with the Air Force. LA life, close to the beach, was good living for both of us; it's one of the reasons employees at RAND tend to stay for a while.

My father would come visit me, and RAND, a few times a year during that period from 2002 to 2004. Sometimes he would come alone; sometimes my mother would tag along.

The first time he met Josh, my father was staying at a modest local airport hotel, and Josh and I offered to pick him up for dinner. Josh was very nervous to meet him. When we got to the hotel, Josh got out of the car to greet Dad. Josh was at least a foot and a half taller than he was, which made for an awkward physical pairing.

However, the two immediately got along well. The point of the conversation wasn't interrogating or vetting Josh, like one might assume when a father meets his daughter's boyfriend; instead, we got into talks about geopolitics, RAND, and the military. Dad had such a deep understanding of global affairs, and he enjoyed talking about these matters—even to his daughter's new boyfriend. He struggled with any sort of small talk and preferred to sit silently if conversations veered into that category. In 2002, I remember the three of us discussing the creation of the Department of Homeland Security. He commented that government reorganizations rarely fix the problem of bureaucracy and lack of interagency communication. Soon thereafter, he would testify to Congress to this effect.

His deep understanding of politics and global affairs was contrasted by zero depth of interest or knowledge in popular culture, which made for some humorous exchanges. At another one of these nice dinners in LA, Mom, Dad, Josh, and I were sitting together, and Josh looked over and said, "Look, there is Rick Fox." (Rick Fox was a very successful basketball player for the Lakers at the time.) My mom and I didn't know who he was, but we looked over and recognized his tablemate, Vanessa Williams.

"Oh, that's Vanessa Williams!" I squealed.

"Who is that?" My dad said.

"I think she was Miss America. She's on TV, Dad," I commented. He looked completely uninterested.

The dinner went on for a while, and thirty minutes later my dad interjected . . . "Oh yeah, she is the one that turns the letters!" My mom, Josh, and I looked at each other quizzically, wondering what the hell my dad was talking about.

Then it finally occurred to Josh. "No, Frank, that's Vanna White."

For Christmas that year, Josh gifted my dad a picture frame from Target with two photos, one with Vanna White and one with Vanessa Williams. It wouldn't be long before my father would be pinning on Josh's new rank of first lieutenant at the Pentagon, and then walking me down the aisle to be married.

By May of 2005, Josh had been at the Pentagon working at a job in the budget office for about six months. He was a first lieutenant, which is a pretty rare sight at the Pentagon, where even captains and majors are considered peons. Upon learning that he was to be promoted to captain, Josh arranged a modest celebration. Because he's not the type to draw attention to himself, and since making captain isn't a big promotion, Josh was trying to downplay the whole thing and not make a big to-do about the ceremony. He asked one of his coworkers to be the MC and he asked his boss, a one-star general, to officiate it. He reserved a small, nondescript conference room, ordered a few party trays from Costco, and brought the drinks for a post-ceremony reception in his unrenovated Pentagon office space on the fifth floor (Josh called it the "attic" of the Pentagon).

Then my whole family came to the ceremony, plus Josh's whole office. It was standing room only. Afterward we all trooped up to Josh's office space with no windows, filled with tiny cubicles. My father stood talking to the general for a few minutes and socialized with others for another ten, about the average length of his preferred social engagement. He then thanked the general for officiating, told Josh it was the first of many promotions to come, and looked around. "So, how do I get out of here?" he asked. "I don't think I've ever been to *this* part of the Pentagon." Josh kindly helped show him out via the third floor, where he was more familiar with his surroundings.

When Josh and I were married in 2007, my father made an exception from his ten-minute socializing timer. He enjoyed himself thoroughly and gave us the following toast.

> Harry Truman once said if you want to give advice to your children, first find out what they want and then advise them to do it. Well, it's been obvious for some time that what Kristin and Josh want is each other, and they didn't need our advice to get married, but we are delighted that they are now Captain and Mrs. Weed. We are particularly pleased to have Josh as a son-in-law. A man of outstanding intellectual achievement, well focused, with a core sense of values and deep compassion and love for Kristin.
>
> As for Kristin, daughters don't come any better. We should all be so lucky. She is warm, she is compassionate, she is outgoing, and she is talented. Like most young children, she went through various phases. First phase is what I would call the "miscellaneous animal phase." We had dogs, rabbits, gerbils, parakeets, goldfish, even worms kept in the bathroom sink. When the first goldfish died, we had to have a burial ceremony in the backyard. The miscellaneous animal phase morphed into the single animal phase—a horse. And it was next to impossible to pry Kristin off of the horse until Josh came along. Josh, I

don't know if you are aware of it, but you were competing against a horse, and we are glad you won . . . [laughter]. Please raise your glasses to many years of life, love and happiness . . .

In the midst of these joyous events were the barely perceptible first signs that my father's final battle had begun, with Parkinson's.

CHAPTER NINE

TWILIGHT

WHEN MY HALF BROTHER and half sister, Chip and Karen, each began having children, and later when I did as well, my father took on a new role—that of "Bumpa." His preferred title was also what we had called our grandfather, his dad, Frank Carlucci II. According to family lore, my niece Marina, my father's first granddaughter, came up with that name for him completely unprompted as a toddler. And so, for the last twenty-five years of his life, my father was no longer "Dad" or "Frank" but delighted in being "Bumpa" to our growing family. Of the many titles he held over the course of his lifetime, only a few are listed on his tombstone at Arlington Cemetery: LT US Navy, Secretary of Defense, US Ambassador, and Beloved Bumpa.

What began as a minor, irritating tremor in his left hand in 2004 resulted in an official diagnosis of Parkinson's. It felt to me like a cruel twist of fate that a man like my father, who spent a good deal of his life taking care of his body, would be diagnosed with a debilitating, incurable illness at the age of seventy-four.

Not only was he devoted to exercise, but he had also always been steadfast in healthy eating. He ate the same breakfast of granola for years; at lunch or dinner he would deprive himself of carb-heavy pasta or pizza and always opt for chicken or fish. Savoring a glass of red wine in the evenings was his one daily indulgence. It was almost as if he spent his life trying to stave off the inevitability of such a diagnosis.

I internally struggled with the injustice of it, but my father allowed himself no scrap of self-pity. He continued to move through life in the early 2000s like he always had: determined, stalwart, and mission focused. He didn't shy away from his diagnosis or find it a reason to be ashamed. Instead, he chose to become a member of the board of directors of the Parkinson's Action Network (which would later become an arm of The Michael J. Fox Foundation for Parkinson's Research).

In 2006 he spoke on the Hill on behalf of H.R. 810, a stem cell research bill designed to allow greater access to federally funded stem cell research. In his testimony he said,

> I've spent a lot of time on the Hill in various capacities, but I'm here today in a capacity that I'd just as soon not be in and that is as a Parkinson's patient, who also serves on the board of the Parkinson's Action Network.
>
> It's a sinking feeling to be diagnosed with an incurable disease. Your instinct is to fight it with all your strength. Much of the struggle is personal, involving time and commitment. But a substantial part is also related to medical science, the advance of medicine. We don't know for certain

> that stem cell science can lead to a cure for Parkinson's, but it would certainly help our understanding of what causes the disease and what its evolution is, and many think it can lead to a reversal of Parkinson's unrelenting degeneration.

H.R. 810, and its counterpart in the Senate, the Stem Cell Research Enhancement Act, were vetoed by President George W. Bush in 2005 and 2007 respectively.

My father's reference to Parkinson's "unrelenting degeneration" was certainly accurate for the way he experienced it. The disease gradually attacked every bit of him: his body, his voice, and eventually his mind. It took years, however, for the disease to slowly overcome him. His strength and fortitude made it such that he lived and lived very well with Parkinson's for over fourteen years. For much of that time he would still visit with his children, swim with his grandchildren. He would play tennis and travel to visit friends and family.

I felt very fortunate that my own children were able to meet and spend time with my father. From 2008 to 2012, Josh and I lived in Europe as he served in the US Air Force at RAF Mildenhall in England and Ramstein Air Base in Germany. The first Thanksgiving we were on our own, so my mom and dad traveled to our small country home in Stetchworth, England, to visit and to join us for a Thanksgiving meal. Since we didn't have a tennis court available for Dad, he tried his hand at our Wii tennis video game. I'll never forget the sight of him bobbing and swinging around our living room. It was not at all the same but did provide a somewhat adequate substitute for him.

In 2010 our first daughter was born at RAF Lakenheath Military Hospital in England. Josh had been deployed in the

Middle East and made it back home only three weeks before she was born. Mom and Dad once again traveled back to England to welcome their fourth grandchild, Amelia, into the world.

In 2011 we took eleven-month-old Amelia with us to Lisbon to meet my parents for the inauguration of the Carlucci American International School of Lisbon (CAISL) in Portugal. We strolled her through the hallway of the school that would bear her grandfather's name in a country she didn't know, on a visit she wouldn't remember. But she sat happily on his lap as he accepted a large pencil with "CAISL" written on its side, and she smiled toothlessly for photographs.

Back in Virginia, my father's days mostly were filled watching my nieces' sports games, attending lunches or dinners with friends, reading books, and, as always, exercise. He also remained on a few boards well into his final years. I'm not sure he ever considered himself fully retired, but his mind and his body were slowing.

In 2012 I realized it was time to come home. My father's health was getting worse, and I wanted to be closer to my family. The Air Force wasn't accommodating; they wanted to send Josh to Alabama for Staff College, so he instead joined the Air Force Reserves and accepted a job in the private sector. And so, I got my wish; we moved back to Virginia with our young daughter and another one on the way.

During those years, my father experienced many of the same symptoms of Parkinson's and the side effects of treatment that so many patients do. Some medications gave him night tremors. His gait became less steady, and his voice grew quieter and quieter.

As my father's struggle with Parkinson's progressed, I began asking him repeatedly to write down his memories and his life story. Others in my family and in his life had long implored him to do so as well, but he was always too busy—and I think unwilling to undertake what felt like a self-serving project. He now began to be more open to the idea, at least of being able to share his experiences with family members who might never have a chance to get to know him or meet him. Some stories, like being stabbed in the Congo or guiding Nixon around Rio, were already the stuff of legend in our family and among some who knew him well, but I worried these and so many others would be lost to history if not captured on paper. My father reluctantly agreed to start a memoir and began a process of dictating his life story. When he had finished recounting his recollections and transcribed and revised them to his satisfaction, he bound a few copies, entitled the book *A Life of Service*, and sent it off to close family members. As far as he was concerned, his work was done. As I now see it, it was only half complete. It's now my responsibility to take it over the finish line.

When reflecting on my father's life and my relationship with him, I go back to a letter I wrote on the occasion of his seventy-fifth birthday, an excerpt of which reads:

> How lucky am I to have borne witness to such a life, about which I have so many feelings I want to express. As I have grown in your shadow, I have witnessed your love and loyalty to family and country. I see it in the people who followed in your shoes, who comment frequently to me on your allegiance to and conviction in principles. People, sometimes in passing, remark on what an honorable person you are. You have inspired me with your intelligence and encouraged me with your perseverance—as I know you have so many other patriots. You are a wonderful

father and grandfather, loyal and loving, who deserves nothing but all of our respect and devotion.

My father's quiet pleasure in routine and ritual helped sustain us through the challenges of his illness. Dad loved the beach, and he kept up the tradition of flying with my mom to his favorite vacation spot of St. Maarten every year, sometimes twice a year. Some combination of us, his children and grandchildren, would join them. Not only were the beaches beautiful, but the tennis was also plentiful, the food was good, and the hotel where he liked to stay was only a few minutes from the airport. Dad loved the consistency of these vacations. Even as the once-luxurious hotel grew a bit worn down over the years, Dad insisted on returning to the same one. Even after a hurricane devastated the place. Every. Single. Year. He came to know some of the staff like family. When my mom would try to convince him to eat at a restaurant on the French side of the island, he would resist. Why bother driving fifteen minutes to the French side when there were perfectly good restaurants right nearby on our Dutch side? In his later years especially, Dad just wanted simple, easy, and familiar.

Our annual Christmas traditions were another source of joy and comfort. The "Carlucci Sing-Along" continues to this day. It's been going on for so long, my mom has come to refer to it as just the "Sing," and it always takes place the Sunday before Christmas.

Before the big day, Mom has green-covered booklets printed with every Christmas song imaginable. That evening there's always a Christmas cocktail party, a buffet dinner (with people perched awkwardly on couches, balancing plates on their laps), and then loud singing commences with a pianist accompanying.

I won't name names, but over the years there have been certain Washingtonians (many of whom I've referenced in these pages) who have delighted in singing loudly and leading holiday tunes from my parents' living room. One person I will mention is Grant Green (who served as assistant secretary of defense for force management and personnel under my father), who would dress up as Santa so believably that he was requested year after year. He would bring in a bag of toys to give out to all the young guests. He did this for me, for my nieces, and most recently for my children. At some point my nieces began a tradition of dancing out the twelve days of Christmas, and a few years ago, my daughters followed suit. Christmas has always been a magical time in the Carlucci home, and Dad basked in the revelry.

In his last years my father began falling a lot and had to make trips to emergency clinics or local hospitals for one- or two-night stays. We started planning local family getaways to the Poconos or to Rehoboth Beach, knowing our time with him was limited but wanting to spend as much time together as a family as we could. We tried to make vacations accessible to him and to the young children in our family. Instead of playing tennis, he would play catch with the tennis ball with my children. And in those years, to my personal delight, he gave up most of his clean eating and started savoring chocolates by the handful.

In 2016 my niece Marina was accepted to Princeton. She remembers how excited he was when she shared the news with him, and how meaningful that connection was to both of them. She recalled,

> My immediate reaction was to drive over to Nana and Bumpa's house [where they lived nearby in McLean]. Those previous couple of weeks Bumpa had not been in

the best shape. I showed up and when I told him, Bumpa stood right up out of his chair; I remember how quickly he jumped up. Quite frankly I was afraid he was going to fall and hurt himself. But I remember vividly how quickly he jumped up with excitement and he hugged me and then tears came to his eyes. That's always going to be one of my most favorite and powerful memories of him. It was in that moment that I knew I was going to go to Princeton. As soon as I saw how overjoyed he was, I knew that it was my destiny to fulfill that legacy that he had left for me.

We went out to dinner to celebrate the next night or the night after that, and he brought his 25th reunion jacket and gave it to me. I still have that blazer of his, and it's kind of funny, since he was a rather small man it actually kind of fits me . . .

When I'd come home from Princeton in my first couple years, I so appreciated having that connection with him, especially when his health was really declining. He couldn't say or do much, but I would come back to visit and say things like, oh yeah, I went to a party in the dorm that you used to live in! I loved being able to bring him back to his Princeton years; I could tell those memories were still so clear for him. That was a gift I could give back to him that I never could have expected.

My mom was always a partner to my father, but toward the end she also became his primary caretaker, with the help of in-home nursing aides. It's a lonely and emotionally draining job and, for the most part, a thankless one. My father had many admirers but not many close friends. In those last months and years, he relied heavily on my mother and other family, especially Chip, who spent many hours caring for him and who also took him to church with his family on Wednesday evenings. I helped out as much as I could. I would come visit, simply to sit next to him. Together we'd sit side by side, looking out at the woods quietly. He would slide his hand over and pat my hand gently. Saying nothing really, but everything all at once.

I'm grateful that my father was able to spend the twilight of his life at home, surrounded by family.

❋❋❋

When he passed away on June 3, 2018, the condolences and reminiscences poured in. Many of them did offer comfort, and also reminded me of the remarkable life my father had lived.

On a muggy day in late June, my father was buried with full military honors at Arlington Cemetery. At the memorial service he was eulogized by General Colin Powell and by Chip, who referenced one of his favorite stories about my father from when Chip was in the Navy and my father had recently retired as secretary of defense.

> During Desert Shield I was a junior officer in the Pentagon, coming off of a long night standing watch. I'm a lieutenant in the Navy. The admiral who was responsible for the Joint Chiefs of Staff's intelligence briefing calls me in and tells me, I've got this briefing at nine o'clock this morning

and I'd like you to give the Navy portion. He then goes on to tell me that the chairman had invited my father to hear the briefing, given everything going on at the time.

I've been up all night. I was about to go home and sleep, but I have to stick around for two more hours. I haven't shaved; my uniform is a mess, but okay. I have to do this. I go into the secretary of defense's briefing area, which is called the Tank. In there I see the Air Force has sent a three-star, the Army a two-star, the Marines a one-star, and the Navy has sent me, an 0-3. I walk into this room of very senior people and step up to the podium to begin. My dad looks up, sees that it's me, and he yells out, "Wait. You're going to brief me?" and bursts out laughing.

One of the most wonderful aspects of working on this project "with" my father has been the opportunity to hear these stories again, or for the first time. I've had a chance to reconnect with people who knew him and loved him, many of whom I haven't been in touch with for years. Some I've never had a chance to meet before. Sadly, a number of the people with whom I would have liked to speak had passed away either before I began or during my work on this book. My father's only sibling, his sister Joan, died a few months into my writing and researching efforts. I am thankful that I did have the chance to sit and talk with Colin Powell two weeks before he died. This was a man who once served as my "babysitter," and then in service to his country became one of most important Americans of the modern era. His devotion to my father was unshakable; it outlived their mortal lives. I'll forever treasure the fact that I had that chance to meet him and talk with him about my father one last time.

My work on this book also offered me an opportunity to reminisce with my family about my father in a way that we wouldn't have otherwise. My family and I enjoyed long talks, trading stories. Like the one about when my father brought me to have a picnic outside his office at the Pentagon one day when I was six or seven. When we finished, an aide asked if we'd had a nice time. My father replied that we had, and then made an offhand comment that it would have been nice to have a bench to sit on. The next day he was at work, looking out his window, and there was a bench in the exact spot on the lawn where we'd been the day before. He found it hilarious, but also embarrassing. My brother remembered him quipping, "Well, you just wave the magic Pentagon wand and there it is. Though it takes them thirty years if you tell them you want a single jet!"

Another favorite story involved the beloved family dog, Salvador. Once my mom, dad, and I went to visit my brother when he was stationed at Little Creek Base near Virginia Beach. We all went out on a boat together and we brought Salvador with us. The boat was commanded by a chief, and several young sailors, who were all more than a little intimidated to have the secretary of defense on board, stood at attention in their dress whites. Still, they all figured we were just going for a leisurely short cruise. When we were about four hundred or five hundred yards offshore, my father decided he wanted to go for a swim.

"Yes, sir."

Mom, Dad, and I all jumped into the water, and Sal decided to follow us. When we were finished, Salvador couldn't climb back on board the boat. He was 115 pounds of wet dog, and he just couldn't make it up the ladder. So, he turned and started swimming for the beach. Everyone on the boat was watching intently;

we were following behind Sal. The chief was mortified, and also terrified at the thought that he was about to be responsible for drowning the secretary of defense's dog. But Sal made it safely to shore, and all ended well.

In researching this book, I combed through historical records in both public and family archives, the latter of which contained thousands and thousands of items, including pictures, handwritten letters, preserved invitations from events attended by figures who have made a profound impact on history, printouts of cables from the 1970s, yellowed newspaper clippings, and all other manner of memorabilia. Some of these were touching, heartfelt—others were hilarious.

From George H. W. Bush, an apology note written because Bush had accidentally demoted my father when he introduced him as deputy secretary of state, rather than as secretary of defense, on November 26, 1997: "What has happened to me, why am I so forgetful. They say the only good thing about the early stages of senility is that you can hide you[r] own Easter Egg. Am I getting there? In any event I apologize for my gross error."[131]

My father replied on December 11, 1997: "Thanks for the note, but it really wasn't necessary. If I had a nickel for every time I had given somebody the wrong title or name I would be richer than Carlyle can ever make me. Moreover, I had more fun as deputy secretary than as secretary!"

From Kissinger, a telegram upon his imminent retirement as secretary of state, dated January 8, 1977. It reads:

> Dear Frank: We have not always been in total agreement during your two years in Lisbon, but I did not want to leave office without telling you how much I valued your

> judgement and integrity. At a time of historic decision for the Portuguese people, you had much to do with the favorable turn of events. You have performed a considerable service, not only for your own country's interests, but for those of the West generally, and I commend you for it. You have my best wishes for a long and distinguished career, and my thanks for a job well done.[132]

From President Reagan, a personal letter on the occasion of my father's resignation as deputy secretary of defense, dated December 6, 1982: "I would like to thank you on behalf of the American people for your long and dedicated service to our country in a variety of key posts . . . I know that in the years ahead you will be able to look back with pride on your significant accomplishments."[133]

From General Powell, a letter in response to an invitation to an event honoring my father, dated December 3, 2009:

> Frank and I have been friends and colleagues for almost forty years. He has been my boss and one of my best mentors. His life of service and dedication has been an inspiration and a model for me to emulate. I am only one of the thousands of people around the world who have been touched and made better by Frank. He is a humanitarian, a superb diplomat, a business leader and a public servant without peer.[134]

One of the tributes that came after my father's death was from one of his successors as secretary of defense, Robert Gates. I found it especially apt and accurate.

Frank Carlucci was an extraordinary public servant. In multiple agencies and departments, through multiple Republican and Democratic presidencies, Frank was a remarkable problem solver—that rare person in Washington who had a magic touch for actually making bureaucracies work effectively. He was not a shouter or a table-pounder; he knew how to quietly motivate people to do their best and had the guts to hold them accountable when they didn't. Frank was usually easygoing, but also tough as nails. You do not run the American Intelligence Community, the NSC and Department of Defense as effectively as Frank did without the hide of a rhinoceros, without knowing how to plant your feet and be immovable, and without the smarts to negotiate the labyrinth of Washington politics and bureaucracy.

Frank worked for highly opinionated, controversial bosses. Always loyal, he nonetheless tempered their instincts and worked diligently to translate their ideas and desires—and their whims—into effective action. On more than a few occasions, Frank found ways gracefully and without drama to channel bad ideas into bureaucratic oblivion. The physical courage Frank demonstrated . . . was matched by his moral and political courage in Washington fighting for policies and decisions he thought to be right and in the best interest of the United States.

As every new president soon discovers, leading any part of the modern American government, getting it to perform effectively and to accomplish the president's agenda is a daunting task—especially in a time of polarized politics and twenty-four-seven cable news coverage. It is not a task

> for amateurs. Every president needs a utility in-fielder like Frank Carlucci for the toughest jobs—tough, professional, skilled, experienced, politically adept but always putting the national interest first, and wickedly funny. Such men and women have always been scarce; they are now an endangered species.
>
> Frank Carlucci's friends and colleagues will miss him greatly, but not nearly so much as the country he loved so deeply and to which he devoted his life.[135]

My father never sought the spotlight, and because of this, many of his more colorful contemporaries are more easily credited and remembered. I feel his legacy should be better recognized—not because I am his daughter, but because in our modern era of bitter partisanship, the way he lived and the manner in which he moved through Washington, under leaders from both sides of the aisle, offer lessons we all can learn from.

I know his impact continues to reverberate in our national policy and among individual people, in both obvious and unusual ways—including among the younger generation. In my research I came across a term paper written recently by a student in Lisbon, Portugal, who chose to tackle the topic of learning about the man after which his school was named. "I immediately asked my family members if they knew of Frank Carlucci and to my surprise all recognized him as not only a key factor in the post years of the '25 de Abril' but a man who truly understood and greatly helped Portugal."[136] My niece Marina recalled that she first found out that her grandfather was a "big deal" not at an official government function on Capitol Hill but when visiting his old high school with him in Wilkes-Barre, Pennsylvania. People came up to him full of emotion to thank him for his efforts in the flood recovery in that community back in 1972. Many residents in the Wyoming Valley were able to stay there and raise their own families in some small part thanks to my father's work to fund relief efforts there.

My great-grandfather, an immigrant stonemason, arrived in America with nothing. He left his legacy in the form of his own handiwork as he helped to construct national landmarks including the immigration station at Ellis Island and the grand staircase to the Memorial Amphitheater at Arlington National Cemetery, completed in 1918. Exactly one hundred years later my father was carried up those stairs to be honored and remembered for his service to our country, on which he left his own indelible mark.

NOTES

1. George C. Wilson, "'Get Me Carlucci' Is the Summons for the Quintessential Survivor," *The Washington Post*, January 14, 1981, https://www.washingtonpost.com/archive/politics/1981/01/14/get-me-carlucci-is-the-summons-for-the-quintessential-survivor/83ddbf3a-26ae-43e8-80b9-da14f67b2659/.
2. Kingsbury-Smith, Article on Frank Carlucci III retiring as deputy secretary of defense, Hearst Feature Service, January 5, 1983.
3. Ronald Reagan, "Remarks at the Swearing-In Ceremony for Frank C. Carlucci as Secretary of Defense," Transcript of speech delivered November 23, 1987, https://www.reaganlibrary.gov/archives/speech/remarks-swearing-ceremony-frank-c-carlucci-secretary-defense.
4. Erin L. Nissley, "Local History: Italian Immigrant Made His Mark on Scranton," *The Times-Tribune*, October 10, 2021, https://www.thetimes-tribune.com/news/local-history/local-history-italian-immigrant-made-his-mark-on-scranton/article_7be7bba1-2e7d-50f3-9a8a-93f6cac03060.html.
5. "Why Anacostia," The House DC, accessed May 23, 2022, https://thehousedc.org/about/why-anacostia/.
6. "Bureau of Near Eastern Affairs (NEA)," U.S. Department of State, accessed May 23, 2022, https://fam.state.gov/FAM/01FAM/01FAM0160.html.
7. For more info: "Suez Crisis," History.com, November 9, 2009, https://www.history.com/topics/cold-war/suez-crisis.
8. "Ambassador Frank Charles Carlucci III – Part 2," The Association for Diplomatic Studies and Training, April 1, 1997, https://www.adst.org/OH%20TOCs/Carlucci,%20Frank%20Charles%20III%20_April%201,%201997_.pdf.
9. Al Kamen, "Looking for a Job as an Ambassador? Do Your Homework and Travel to That Country," *The Washington Post*, February 11, 2014, https://www.washingtonpost.com/politics/looking-for-a-job-as-an-ambassador-do-your-homework-and-travel-to-that-country/2014/02/11/58e88216-9349-11e3-84e1-27626c5ef5fb_story.html.

10. *Faces and Voices of the United States Abroad: Diversity at U.S. Foreign Affairs Agencies*, Congressional Research Service, January 21, 2021, https://crsreports.congress.gov/product/pdf/R/R46660.
11. Carlucci specifically mentions Amb. Byroade in his interview: "Ambassador Frank Charles Carlucci III – Part 2," The Association for Diplomatic Studies and Training.
12. *South African Statistics, 2012*, Statistics South Africa, 2012, table on p. 26, https://www.statssa.gov.za/publications/SAStatistics/SAStatistics2012.pdf.
13. *Encyclopaedia Britannica Online,* Academic ed., s.v. "African National Congress," accessed May 23, 2022, https://www.britannica.com/topic/African-National-Congress.
14. *Encyclopaedia Britannica Online*, Academic ed., s.v. "Pass law," accessed May 23, 2022, https://www.britannica.com/topic/pass-law.
15. "The Pan-African Congress - A New African Political Organization," Foreign Service Dispatch, April 17, 1959.
16. "Ambassador Frank Charles Carlucci III – Part 2," The Association for Diplomatic Studies and Training.
17. For more information on the Congo Free State: *Encyclopaedia Britannica Online,* Academic ed., s.v. "Congo Free State," accessed May 23, 2022, https://www.britannica.com/place/Congo-Free-State.
18. For more information on the Belgian Congo: *Encyclopaedia Britannica Online*, Academic ed., s.v. "Belgian Congo," accessed May 23, 2022, https://www.britannica.com/place/Belgian-Congo.
19. "Ambassador Frank Charles Carlucci III – Part 2," The Association for Diplomatic Studies and Training.
20. "City Native Assumes Post in Zanzibar," *The Scranton Tribune*, February 25, 1964.
21. For further reading on the Congo at this time, see *Overtime in Heaven: Adventures in the Foreign Service* by Peter Lisagor and Marguerite Higgins.
22. "The Congo, Decolonization, and the Cold War, 1960–1965," Office of the Historian, accessed May 23, 2022, https://history.state.gov/milestones/1961–1968/congo-decolonization.
23. "Ambassador Frank Charles Carlucci III – Part 2," The Association for Diplomatic Studies and Training, p. 36.
24. "Ambassador Frank Charles Carlucci III – Part 2," The Association for Diplomatic Studies and Training.
25. Jack Rosenthal, "Antipoverty Nominee," *New York Times*, December 31, 1970, https://www.nytimes.com/1970/12/31/archives/antipoverty-nominee-frank-charles-carlucci-3d.html.
26. "Ambassador Frank Charles Carlucci III – Part 2," The Association for Diplomatic Studies and Training.
27. "Ambassador Frank Charles Carlucci III – Part 2," The Association for Diplomatic Studies and Training.
28. "Carlucci Aids New Nation," *Thursday Evening Post*, Wilkes-Barre, 1965.

29. Liz Dee, "'You're Outta Here!': Getting Declared Persona Non Grata," Association for Diplomatic Studies and Training, July 17, 2014, https://adst.org/2014/07/youre-outta-here/.

30. Marie Ridder, "Where Is Carlucci? Coming to Grips with Radical Revolution out in a Difficult, Changing World," *Washingtonian Magazine*.

31. Cable from Gordon about Brazil: "183. Telegram From the Embassy in Brazil to the Department of State," Office of the Historian, accessed May 23, 2022, https://history.state.gov/historicaldocuments/frus1964-68v31/d183.

32. "João Goulart," Brown University Library, accessed May 23, 2022, https://library.brown.edu/create/fivecenturiesofchange/chapters/chapter-6/presidents/joao-goulart/.

33. "Kennedy and Goulart," Brown University Library, accessed May 23, 2022, https://library.brown.edu/create/wecannotremainsilent/chapters/chapter-1-revolution-and-counterrevolution-in-brazil/kennedy-and-goulart/.

34. "Operation Topsy" *Foreign Policy* no. 8 (Autumn 1972): pp. 62–85.

35. Jack Corrigan and Government Executive, "The Hollowing-Out of the State Department Continues," *The Atlantic*, February 11, 2018, https://www.theatlantic.com/international/archive/2018/02/tillerson-trump-state-foreign-service/553034/.

36. Ridder, "Where Is Carlucci?"

37. Georgia Martinez, "Proud Couple Watch Nixon Name Son OEO Chief," *The Miami Herald*, December 12, 1970.

38. "Press Conference of Frank Carlucci, Director, Office of Economic Opportunity," The White House, May 5, 1971.

39. Jack Rosenthal, "Panel Appointed in Legal Aid Case," *New York Times*, March 27, 1971.

40. "Ronald Reagan Oral History Project," Miller Center of Public Affairs, University of Virginia, August 28, 2001, https://millercenter.org/the-presidency/presidential-oral-histories/frank-carlucci-oral-history.

41. Stanford News Service, "George Shultz, Statesman and Stanford Scholar, Dies at 100," *Stanford News*, February 7, 2021, https://news.stanford.edu/2021/02/07/george-shultz-statesman-stanford-scholar-dies-100/.

42. Philip Taubman, "The Shultz-Weinberger Feud," *New York Times Magazine*, April 14, 1985, https://www.nytimes.com/1985/04/14/magazine/the-shultz-weinberger-feud.html.

43. "Ambassador Frank Charles Carlucci III – Part 2," The Association for Diplomatic Studies and Training, pp. 68–70.

44. *Natural Disaster Survey Report 73-1*, U.S. Department of Commerce, National Oceanic and Atmospheric Association, February 1973, https://www.weather.gov/media/publications/assessments/Hurricane%20Agnes%201972.pdf.

45. "Hurricane Agnes - 45 Years Later," Northeast Regional Climate Center, Cornell University, accessed May 23, 2022, https://www.nrcc.cornell.edu/services/blog/2017/06/20/index.html.

46. Robert P. Wolensky, *Better Than Ever: The Flood Recovery Task Force and the 1972 Agnes Disaster* (Stevens Point: University of Wisconsin-Stevens Point Foundation Press, 1993).
47. Erin L. Nissey, "Local History: Italian Immigrant Made His Mark on Scranton," *The Times-Tribune*, October 10, 2021, https://www.thetimes-tribune.com/news/local-history/local-history-italian-immigrant-made-his-mark-on-scranton/article_7be7bba1-2e7d-50f3-9a8a-93f6cac03060.html.
48. Dana Hedgpeth, "The Week Hundreds of Native Americans Took Over D.C.'s Bureau of Indian Affairs," *The Washington Post*, January 24, 2021, https://www.washingtonpost.com/history/2021/01/24/native-americans-occupied-bureau-indian-afffairs-nixon/.
49. "Ambassador Frank Charles Carlucci III – Part 2," The Association for Diplomatic Studies and Training, p. 70.
50. "Ambassador Frank Charles Carlucci III – Part 2," The Association for Diplomatic Studies and Training, p. 76.
51. "Frank Carlucci," Gerald R. Ford Foundation, pp. 6–7, September 4, 2009, https://geraldrfordfoundation.org/centennial/oralhistory/frank-carlucci/.
52. "Frank Carlucci," Gerald R. Ford Foundation, p. 12.
53. John Garon, correspondence and interview with the author, September 2021.
54. Ridder, "Where Is Carlucci?"
55. Ridder, "Where Is Carlucci?"
56. Barry Hatton, "Mário Soares, Portugal's Former President and PM, Dies at 92," AP News, January 7, 2017, https://apnews.com/article/fc7a00d5a44643c9a8df15a25162b6da.
57. For further reading on this time period, see *Carlucci Versus Kissinger* by Bernardino Gomes and Tiago Moreira de Sa.
58. John Garon, correspondence and interview with the author, September 2021.
59. *Foreign Relations of the United States, 1969–1979*, ed. Kathleen B. Rasmussen, volume E-15, Part 2, "Documents on Western Europe," *1973–1976* (United States Government Publishing Office, 2021), https://static.history.state.gov/frus/frus1969
-76ve15p2Ed2/pdf/frus1969-76ve15p2Ed2.pdf.
60. John Garon, correspondence and interview with the author, September 2021.
61. Jamie Smith, "Frank Carlucci: Helping Block the Communists in Portugal," The Association for Diplomatic Studies and Training, June 7, 2018, https://adst.org/2018/06/frank-carlucci-helping-block-the-communists-in-portugal.
62. "Ambassador Frank Charles Carlucci III – Part 1," The Association for Diplomatic Studies and Training, April 1, 1997, p. 5, https://www.adst.org/OH%20TOCs/Carlucci,%20Frank%20Charles%20III.toc.pdf.
63. "Ambassador Frank Charles Carlucci III – Part 1," The Association for Diplomatic Studies and Training.

64. *The Secretary of State's Register of Culturally Significant Property 2019*, Bureau of Overseas Building Operations, September 2019, https://www.state.gov/wp-content/uploads/2020/04/SecReg_2018-2019_web.pdf.

65. George Glass, "The Residence of the U.S. Ambassador to Portugal Is Now Casa Carlucci," Transcript of speech delivered September 6, 2019, https://pt.usembassy.gov/residence-of-the-u-s-ambassador-to-portugal-is-casa-carlucci/.

66. "Paratroop Mutiny: The Situation as of Evening Nov 26," U.S. Embassy in Lisbon, November 26, 1975, https://www.wikileaks.org/plusd/cables/1975LISBON07084_b.html.

67. Bernardino Gomes and Tiago Moreira de Sá, *Carlucci versus Kissinger* (Lexington Books, 2011), p. 117.

68. "360. Memorandum From the President's Assistant for National Security Affairs (Scowcroft) to President Ford," Office of the Historian, November 29, 1975, https://history.state.gov/historicaldocuments/frus1969-76ve15p2Ed2/d360.

69. "Casa Carlucci," U.S. Embassy Portugal, YouTube, video, https://www.youtube.com/watch?v=ToNvSP4BZac.

70. Glass, "The Residence of the U.S. Ambassador to Portugal."

71. "Gerald R. Ford Oral History Project: Frank Carlucci," Gerald Ford Foundation, September 4, 2009, https://geraldrfordfoundation.org/centennial/oralhistory/frank-carlucci/.

72. John Garon, correspondence and interview with the author, September 2021.

73. "Under Secretaries of State for Management," Office of the Historian, accessed May 23, 2022, https://history.state.gov/departmenthistory/people/principalofficers/under-secretary-for-mgmt.

74. Scott Neuman, "Stansfield Turner, Who Headed CIA Under Carter, Dies at 94," NPR, January 19, 2018, https://www.npr.org/sections/thetwo-way/2018/01/19/579062737/stansfield-turner-who-headed-cia-under-carter-dies-at-94.

75. Michael Bold, "Then and Now - Carlucci Initiatives," U.S. Army, September 14, 2016, https://www.army.mil/article/174478/then_and_now_carlucci_initiatives.

76. Bold, "Then and Now."

77. "Oral History Interview with Frank Carlucci," Office of the Secretary of Defense, April 12, 1989.

78. Kingsbury-Smith, Hearst Newspapers.

79. "Ambassador Frank Charles Carlucci III – Part 2," The Association for Diplomatic Studies and Training, p. 84.

80. Robert M. Gates, "A Tribute to Frank Carlucci," National Academy of Public Administration, https://napawash.org/uploads/A_Tribute_to_Frank_Carlucci.pdf.

81. Colin Powell, interview with the author, October 4, 2021.

82. Ronald Reagan, "Address to the Nation on Defense and National Security," Reagan Foundation, March 23, 1983, https://www.reaganfoundation.org/media/128846/nation4.pdf.

83. "Intermediate-Range Nuclear Forces Treaty (INF Treaty), 1987," U.S. Department of State Archive, https://2001-2009.state.gov/r/pa/ho/time/rd/104266.htm.

84. "Ambassador Frank Charles Carlucci III – Part 2," The Association for Diplomatic Studies and Training, p. 91.

85. Nicholas Lemann, "Escape Artist: The Carlucci Technique," *The New Republic*, August 1, 1988.

86. Helen Dewar and Margot Hornblower, "Two Republican Senators Vote Against Weinberger," *The Washington Post*, January 21, 1981, https://www.washingtonpost.com/archive/politics/1981/01/21/two-republican-senators-vote-against-weinberger/f6d7b881-cad7-4974-bafc-7131ee10098a/.

87. Philip Taubman, "The Shultz-Weinberger Feud," *New York Times*, April 14, 1985, https://www.nytimes.com/1985/04/14/magazine/the-shultz-weinberger-feud.html.

88. "Ambassador Frank Charles Carlucci III – Part 1," The Association for Diplomatic Studies and Training.

89. "Caspar W. Weinberger," Historical Office, Office of the Secretary of Defense, accessed May 23, 2022, https://history.defense.gov/Multimedia/Biographies/Article-View/Article/571286/caspar-w-weinberger/.

90. "The 1992 Pardons," Understanding the Iran-Contra Affairs, Brown University, accessed May 23, 2022, https://www.brown.edu/Research/Understanding_the_Iran_Contra_Affair/thepardons.php.

91. "Ambassador Frank Charles Carlucci III – Part 2," The Association for Diplomatic Studies and Training, p. 97.

92. Colin Powell, interview with the author, October 4, 2021.

93. "Ambassador Frank Charles Carlucci III – Part 2," The Association for Diplomatic Studies and Training, p. 95.

94. William Howard Taft IV, interview with the author, September 15, 2021.

95. "Oral History Interview with Frank Carlucci – Part 6," Office of the Secretary of Defense, April 12, 1989.

96. Eric Yoder, "Carlucci Departs. His Curtain Speech: Honor the Producers," *Federal Times*, January 10, 1983.

97. "Ambassador Frank Charles Carlucci III – Part 2," The Association for Diplomatic Studies and Training, p. 97.

98. Robert D. McFadden, "Frank C. Carlucci, Diplomat and Defense Secretary to Reagan, Dies at 87," *New York Times*, June 4, 2018, nytimes.com/2018/06/04/obituaries/frank-carlucci-dead.html.

99. "Ambassador Frank Charles Carlucci III – Part 2," The Association for Diplomatic Studies and Training, p. 94.

100. "Ronald Reagan Oral History Project," Miller Center of Public Affairs.

101. "Operation Illwind," FBI – Famous Cases & Criminals, accessed May 23, 2022, https://www.fbi.gov/history/famous-cases/operation-illwind.

102. "Operation Illwind," FBI – Famous Cases & Criminals.

103. "Base Closure and Realignment (BRAC): Background and Issues for Congress," Congressional Research Service, April 25, 2019, https://sgp.fas.org/crs/natsec/R45705.pdf.

104. "Oral History Interview with Frank Carlucci – Part 5," Office of the Secretary of Defense, April 12, 1989.

105. "Frank C. Carlucci," Historical Office, Office of the Secretary of Defense, accessed May 23, 2022, https://history.defense.gov/Multimedia/Biographies/Article-View/Article/571285/frank-c-carlucci/.

106. Bill Owens, interview with the author, October 2, 2021.

107. "Topics of the Times; From Russia with Apologies," *New York Times*, June 16, 1988, https://www.nytimes.com/1988/06/16/opinion/topics-of-the-times-from-russia-with-apologies.html.

108. "Topics of the Times; From Russia with Apologies," *New York Times*.

109. "The Intermediate-Range Nuclear Forces (INF) Treaty at a Glance," Arms Control Association, August 2019, https://www.armscontrol.org/factsheets/INFtreaty.

110. Vincent J. Schodolski and *Chicago Tribune*, "Soviet Strategy Troubles Carlucci," *Chicago Tribune*, August 3, 1988, https://www.chicagotribune.com/news/ct-xpm-1988-08-03-8801200093-story.html.

111. Philip Taubman, "Carlucci Is Skeptical; Is the Soviet Military on the Gorbachev Diet?" *New York Times*, August 7, 1988, https://www.nytimes.com/1988/08/07/weekinreview/the-world-carlucci-is-skeptical-is-the-soviet-military-on-the-gorbachev-diet.html.

112. Andrew R. Marvin, "Operation Earnest Will—The U.S. Foreign Policy behind U.S. Naval Operations in the Persian Gulf 1987–89; A Curious Case," *Naval War College Review* (Spring 2020), https://digital-commons.usnwc.edu/cgi/viewcontent.cgi?article=8115&context=nwc-review.

113. "Operation Praying Mantis," Naval History and Heritage Command, accessed May 23, 2022, https://www.history.navy.mil/browse-by-topic/wars-conflicts-and-operations/middle-east/praying-mantis.html.

114. Lemann, "Escape Artist: The Carlucci Technique."

115. "Frank C. Carlucci," Historical Office, Office of the Secretary of Defense.

116. George J. Church, "Bringing the Pentagon to Heel," *TIME*, June 20, 1988.

117. Oliver Burkeman and Julian Borger, "The Ex-presidents' Club," *The Guardian*, September 11, 2001, https://www.theguardian.com/world/2001/oct/31/september11.usa4.

118. David Rubenstein, interview with the author, April 24, 2022.

119. Terence O'Hara, "Carlyle Shows It's Still Tops with Defense Deal," NBC News, February 13, 2006, https://www.nbcnews.com/id/wbna11324989.

120. Michael Lewis, "The Access Capitalists," *The New Republic*, October 18, 1993, https://newrepublic.com/article/74485/the-access-capitalists.

121. Greg Schneider, "Gerstner to Be Carlyle Group Chairman," *The Washington Post*, November 22, 2002, https://www.washingtonpost.com/archive/business/2002/11/22/gerstner-to-be-carlyle-group-chairman/466ad0b8-9f3f-4497-b2a3-94856215cd1e/.

122. Greg Schneider, "Connections and Then Some," *The Washington Post*, March 16, 2003, https://www.washingtonpost.com/archive/lifestyle/2003/03/16/connections-and-then-some/faaece9e-0225-4310-a8f9-8137d2329d52/.

123. "Statement on the Passing of Frank Carlucci," The Carlyle Group, June 4, 2018, https://www.carlyle.com/media-room/news-release-archive/statement-passing-frank-carlucci.

124. "PEI 300," Private Equity International, accessed May 23, 2022, https://www.privateequityinternational.com/database/#/pei-300.

125. "Our Firm," The Carlyle Group, accessed May 23, 2022, https://www.carlyle.com/#our-firm.

126. Kathleen Day, "Frank Carlucci and the Corporate Whirl," *The Washington Post*, February 7, 1993, https://www.washingtonpost.com/archive/business/1993/02/07/frank-carlucci-and-the-corporate-whirl/76cc1649-0575-4357-9aa5-5eb9cb296ebb/.

127. Day, "Frank Carlucci and the Corporate Whirl."

128. "A Brief History of RAND," RAND Corporation, accessed May 24, 2022, https://www.rand.org/about/history.html.

129. Peter Reuter, Gordon Crawford, Jonathan Cave, Patrick Murphy, Don Henry, William Lisowski, and Eleanor Sullivan Wainstein, *Sealing the Borders: The Effects of Increased Military Participation in Drug Interdiction*, RAND Corporation, 1988, https://www.rand.org/pubs/reports/R3594.html.

130. Michael Rich, interview with the author, January 20, 2022.

131. George H. W. Bush, letter to Frank Carlucci, November 26, 1997.

132. Henry Kissinger, telegram to Frank Carlucci, January 8, 1977.

133. Ronald Reagan, letter to Frank Carlucci, December 6, 1982.

134. Colin Powell, letter to Frank Carlucci, December 3, 2009.

135. Robert Gates, personal correspondence.

136. Rogerio Leitao, Grade 11.

INDEX

ABOUT *the* AUTHORS

KRISTIN CARLUCCI WEED grew up in McLean, Virginia, as the daughter of former Secretary of Defense Frank C. Carlucci III. Weed attended Duke University and Johns Hopkins University, focusing on international affairs and public policy. After working in policy research in the US and in Europe, she returned to the leafy suburbs of Washington, DC, where she settled with her US Air Force husband in 2020. When she is not driving one of her three children to their activities, she can be found on the tennis court or planning her next globetrotting adventure.

Get Me Carlucci is her first book.

FRANK C. CARLUCCI III was an American politician and diplomat. A graduate of the Princeton School of Public and International Affairs, Carlucci served as ambassador to Portugal in the tumultuous 1970s and held roles in a number of public offices, including at the Office of Economic Opportunity and the Central Intelligence Agency. As President Ronald Reagan's secretary of defense from

1987 to 1989, Carlucci helped define America's Cold War policy. In private enterprise, he was chairman of The Carlyle Group from 1992 to 2003.

Before his death in 2018, Carlucci completed a draft of his memoir, which serves as the basis for *Get Me Carlucci*.